DAVID ROCHE

Standing at the Back Door of Happiness

And How I Unlocked It

T0321298

HARBOUR PUBLISHING

Harbour Publishing Co. Ltd.
P.O. Box 219, Madeira Park, BC, V0N 2H0
www.harbourpublishing.com

Edited by Arlene Prunkl
Cover and text design by Dwayne Dobson
Printed and bound in Canada
Printed on 100% recycled paper

Harbour Publishing acknowledges the support of the Canada Council for the Arts, the Government of Canada, and the Province of British Columbia through the BC Arts Council.

Library and Archives Canada Cataloguing in Publication

Title: Standing at the back door of happiness : and how I unlocked it / David Roche.
Names: Roche, David (Motivational speaker), author.
Identifiers: Canadiana (print) 20240298071 | Canadiana (ebook) 20240298349 | ISBN 9781990776762 (softcover) | ISBN 9781990776779 (EPUB)
Subjects: LCSH: Roche, David (Motivational speaker) |
  LCSH: Disfigured persons—Canada—Biography. |
  LCSH: Face—Abnormalities—Patients—Canada—Biography. |
  LCSH: Motivational speakers—Canada—Biography. |
  LCSH: Humorists, Canadian—Biography. |
  LCSH: Happiness. | LCSH: Self-acceptance. |
  LCGFT: Autobiographies.
Classification: LCC RD763 .R63 2024 | DDC 362.4092—dc23

Standing at the Back Door
of Happiness

To Artie Noble,
who told me when we were both thirteen
that I was a great writer.

Contents

Acknowledgements

I have been carried into this very moment on the shoulders of others. Your names are too many to mention here, but your hearts fill this page. You range from my family of birth to my chosen family, from dearest friends to appreciative audiences, and to you who are readers. Thank you for helping me step through the back door of happiness.

Introduction

I was born with a vascular malformation. The veins in the left side of my face, head, neck, throat and tongue have grown and grown throughout my life. My lower lip was removed at the Mayo Clinic in 1945 when I was fifteen months old.

Despite what most people are inclined to think when they first meet me, my facial difference has been an incredible gift because I have been forced to look inside myself to find my beauty and sense of self-worth. That gift has given birth to a second one: I can see the beauty of other people, as flawed as we all are. I live (mostly) in a world of beautiful people.

That is, of course, a rather facile statement. I toss around the word *beauty* with little compunction. The full truth is more layered and complex. Finding my own beauty came slowly, the realizations often accompanied by a grinding noise, but when the realization was an epiphany, the sound was more like an angelic chorus.

The stories, essays, memoirettes, letters and other pieces in this volume are about the journey of finding and nurturing that positive sense of myself and encouraging it in others. Some parts of that journey were years long, others evanescent. A few arced across my entire life. Some surprised me, others stepped into my life gradually, like the slow emergence of Michelangelo's *David* from raw marble. What links them is an exploration of the revelation of the beauty of others and of myself.

One recurring theme is death. The process of dying is profoundly revelatory of beauty of all sorts. There is such a thing as "a good death," but even those good deaths are raw, at times fractious, smelly, scary. But they are always, always beautiful.

This volume also includes *cri de cœur* pieces wherein you may find my deep messiah complex juxtaposed with some sincere, heartfelt messages to the world. I attended a Roman Catholic seminary where I studied to be a priest for four years; hence, I have a tendency to sermonize (some would say rant). My hope—actually, my belief—is that some important truths are embedded there for you.

You will see families, both by birth and by choice, appear in my writing. I was born into a household consisting of my mother, her two younger sisters, my maternal grandparents, and Blackie the dog. As the first grandchild, I was cherished and nurtured, especially because it was wartime and my father was in Stalag 17. My second family came to me through my love for my wife, Marlena.

I have always been drawn to environments characterized by service and community. This book is replete with both. You will read of how my growth, my joy, and most of the choices made by my heart were woven by and into the lives of others.

A particular joy for me has been my involvement with storytelling, both as a performer and a coach. I have a special insight into the beauty of others as they express their truths and reveal that beauty. I can hear the truth their souls are expressing even when they think their spoken words are what count.

Much of what I have written is self-referential, but that self has a highly developed social nervous system. I am relational: I seek healing, love and understanding in the company of others. It flows both ways—I want ENCOURAGER carved on my tombstone.

I have an inner life that is highly imaginative, but I rarely dwell on myself alone. I am one of seven children. In the seminary I shared a large dorm room with fifty other adolescent boys. I always had roommates in college, and after graduation I lived with three roommates until I got married. After my first marriage and divorce I shared an apartment with three gay men. I had never slept in a room of my own until I was twenty-eight. I spent eight years in a co-operative working environment and twelve years as a communist organizer. All my work, including as a computer programmer, involved strong links to others. I was one of the co-founders of the Childcare Switchboard and Single Parent Resource Center of San Francisco, where we worked co-operatively for eight years. The twelve years I spent as a Marxist-Leninist cadre were group-oriented in the extreme. Even during my thirty-plus years as a solo performer and public speaker, I was always enmeshed with the audience.

I am commonly viewed as being inspiring and happy, with a wonderful sense of humour. All true. But I have carried anger inside me, often with little understanding of its birthplace. This book can be read as the story of that inner anger's diminution, its relegation to being a little-used and less-valued emotion, although always present. I have to some degree been able to channel and focus that darker energy to act in the service of my heart.

So many people have held open that door to happiness for me. Love comes in infinite varieties, like a store with a bulk "love" aisle. Come with me. Find and sample love as I have.

For the Love of Scars

J amie's scar, as big as my hand, was shiny and strong, stretching across her belly. I think she wanted to show it to me because I have visible scars; she had a secret one that she could keep hidden but chose to show me as a gesture of solidarity or camaraderie. She pulled up her t-shirt and it gleamed iridescent there in the sun, with the sheen of a dragonfly wing, a moonstone.

As I stared, somehow my heart opened. Why would that be? A human bond of shared suffering, shared history of surgery and pain? A mutual trust based on an intimate moment?

I looked at Jamie's face. She was looking down, like a child being scolded. I glanced away, not wanting to embarrass her. Then I had to look back, and she looked into my eyes. What did she want? Her eyes flickered, also iridescent. She just wanted the moment, and I gave it to her. And she gave it to me. Then she looked down again. No need to talk.

The truth is, your body loves scars. Your flesh cleaves to

scars, needs them near at hand and ready to help. Just look at how the surrounding flesh embraces your scar. So then you feel embarrassed about them? Hey, you grew that scar yourself! You did it. It's part and parcel of you. And I know you play with your scar. I know you feel around the edges and press into the place where it hurts good.

I liked to touch the edges of my friend Sarah's mastectomy scar. The area around the incision still had sensitivity. It held the memory of her breast. Some of the surrounding areas were irritable, painful where there was a tug or push against a nerve. Other places were numb. Others were half and half. Her scar was not a foreign body, not an intrusion, not an unwelcome guest. It was a latecomer to Sarah's being, but no matter, it was still Sarah.

Scars stand out because they are proud of who they are.

Scars are the adopted children in the family of flesh. Scars have souls. And feelings. Scars can form around nerve tissue. They protect the nerve tissue. Scars do that so they can have feelings. They are *feeling parasites*.

When I was teaching a storytelling class, Merijane announced her story's title was "A Good Mastectomy." Telling this story for the first time, she spoke with compelling ease, and as she neared the end, she gestured to the left side of her chest and then rested her hand there in a lovely grace note. We were all still. My instincts led me to ask, "Would you like to show us your scar?" She did. It was a perfect scar, a perfect end to her story, and a revelation of the beauty of scars.

All scars are charged at their birth with responsibility, pledged to hold firm, with a sense of duty to the tissues they have come to heal.

A scar has its own memory. A memory of responsibility and hard work. A memory of being there day after day, often unappreciated. You will never hear a scar whine.

Scars have helped to form my personality. They are how I developed my rigidity. Yes, a scar has a certain rigidity. And tenderness around the edges. Just like me.

They also have elasticity. They change, just like the rest of our bodies, only more slowly. Not with abandon, but with attention to duty. I can see why I am attracted to scars. Because I too hold on tight to my sense of place and resist change. I love the dependability of scars.

Wounds heal from the edges. The scab forms. When it falls away, the scar is in the middle. It holds the centre, it holds its place.

Scars are the military of the body; they report to the immune system. This is not juicy, hydrated tissue, not smooth skin or slippery mucous membrane. This is collagen—nature's rebar.

Scars are about healing. Scars are about forgiveness. Scars help us forget pain and loss.

There are other kinds of scars besides those on our bodies. Every marriage, every relationship that endures, has scars. Some call these *emotional scars*. They are evidence of healing. People who cannot endure the pain that comes with relationships will run away from wounds and will never scar. But their wounds still bleed. They need scar love. Love that heals wounds. Love that endures.

Night and Day

Those of us who are perceived as having disabilities have great lessons to bring into the world. When students ask me, as they often do, how I learned to be confident and find my inner beauty, I tend to shrug and say that it was given to me. But I sometimes find, afterward, that I am not satisfied with that short answer. In truth, I want to tell twelve-year-olds how they can learn to believe in themselves and their own beauty. This story is an exploration of that mystery.

Let's go back to 217 Conkey Street in Hammond, Indiana, in the summer of 1951, for a deep love story.

I am visiting my grandparents. I don't have to be in bed until 10:30, lots later than at home. I don't tell the other kids because they might tell Mom and Dad.

Nana says I am King David and my bed is the royal bed. The sheets are very slippery. She says they are royal satin sheets. The bed is funny. I like my bed at home better. It goes down in the middle; when I'm alone I can stay down there and sleep. At Nana's house the bed goes up in the middle, and I slide off the slippery sheets. I have to push my foot and my hand between the bed and the wall and hold on to the bed so I won't slide. I think, *Maybe kings and queens have to sleep this way.*

I was King David because I was born in 1944 while my father was a prisoner of war in the Nazis' Stalag Luft 17 B camp in Austria. I was the first child and the first grandchild, arriving into a family consisting of my grandmother (the matriarch), my grandfather Frank, my teenaged aunts Dorothy and Jane, and of course my mother, Virginia. And Blackie the dog. During a time of war and fear and deprivation I appeared, a treasured gift. My aunt Nancy had died some years previously, and her loss was grievous for Nana. I know I replaced Nancy in some way, although the pain of the death of a child never fully abates.

I don't go to sleep right away. I hear the TV in the living room. Nana lets me keep the door open a little bit. She thinks I am afraid at night, but I am not afraid. I just like to listen. Nana laughs louder than Frank, but they both have a nice laugh. I feel like I am visiting with them, and I laugh to myself in bed when I hear them.

The light from the TV is different from other light; it's more grey. I can't tell what they are saying on TV, but I like the sound. Mostly I like listening to Nana and Frank talk, even though I can't understand them. Their voices become dreamy as I drowse. I feel loved.

I now understand that simply feeling the cadence and tone of their voices was indeed a form of love.

I smell Frank's cigar. I can't tell what kind it is by the smell. I'd have to see the box or the cigar band; there is one on every cigar. Frank likes two kinds: White Owls and Dutch Masters. White Owls have a white owl on the box and Dutch Masters have a nice old painting of the Dutch masters guys with their costumes on. I am given the boxes for my baseball cards or pencils at school.

I like it when he smokes White Owls because they sponsor the White Sox games on WCFL, "the voice of labour in Chicago." When one of the White Sox hits a home run, Bob Elson says, "That's a White Owl wallop and a box of White Owl cigars goes to Sherman Lollar" or whoever hit the home run.

I don't have a nightlight. I don't need one. I am not afraid at night. I like it here. Light peeks in the windows from cars sometimes. I can tell when there is a car in the alley across the street because the light gets bright and then it moves away. I hear all the cars going by, and their sound blends with the house. I ride the sounds and lights into the dream world.

The first morning smell is of the pillow. As I come awake, I know I am not at home because the first smell there is pee from Kevin's bedwetting.

Sharing a bed with Kev meant getting used to clinging to the side of the bed to avoid rolling down into the centre depression. That was his territory by default. He rolled down there and peed, and anyone else sharing the bed was half out of it trying to keep away from the pee pool. You kind of got used to it. It wasn't that bad, really—it was preparation for old age and incontinence, though I didn't know that back then.

The pillow smell at Nana's house is Tide detergent, strong, clean and chemical. I associate it with her, and I love it.

High heels click and work boots clump on the sidewalk in front, no doubt heading down Conkey to Hohman Avenue for the bus stop to downtown Hammond. The breeze brings in other smells. Diesel buses out on Hohman Avenue fart thick black exhaust, and it drifts toward the house.

The smell of diesel exhaust was so prevalent in my life that, as stenchy as most people consider it to be, even today it still brings me back home. The air always had an industrial smell, especially when the wind came from the north, off Lake Michigan. The window of our upstairs bedroom at home provided a good view of the industrial pollution taking place at Standard Oil, Inland Steel, US Steel, Youngstown Sheet and Tube and all the other industries that made this corner of northwest Indiana the most polluted place on the planet. There was an eerie beauty to it. The refineries released waste gases into 150-foot-tall chimneys and they burned at the top like monstrous torches. Slag dumped at the mills blushed brilliantly against night skies. We had eternal dawn all night long, year round.

At Nana and Frank's, the scent of new-mown grass from old Mr. Funk's house next door blends with the diesel exhaust. He always mows in the same way: the hand mower pushed chattering ahead for five seconds, stopping for three seconds, then another five-second push ahead and a three-second rest, going five, resting three, until he comes to the corner of the yard and turns. Around again, smaller and smaller, until he's done in the middle. I wonder why he mows the lawn so often. Nana says he just likes to do it. Then the sprinkler, at first with a sputter, then in rhythm: *shew, shew, shew, shew,* then *ch, ch, ch, ch, ch, ch.*

I kneel at the window and watch Mr. Funk. He always wears tan pants and a short-sleeved white shirt and a straw hat and glasses. He watches the sprinkler and then surprises me with his sudden graceful snapping of the hose like a whip to move the sprinkler to the next watering spot.

I stick my tongue out to taste the smell of the grass. I press my nose against the screen; it smells of rusty metal. The breeze rattles the dusty blinds. Three dead flies lie on the sill between the window and the screen. An ant, one of the big black ones, marches across the screen.

The aroma of coffee drifts in from the other end of the house, and I turn to listen. I know where Nana is—at the stove. Coffee is being boiled in a large, enamelled coffeepot with Pennsylvania Dutch decorations. She always puts egg-shells in the coffee. She told me why, but I didn't understand.

I go into the living room quietly, and I stop to check the leavings of the previous evening. Yes, a White Owl cigar butt lies in the big green ashtray. I slide the band off and onto my finger. I pick up Nana's sherry glass and smell it—another aroma, sweet and entrancing, that grounds and comforts me. I tip a leftover couple of drops into my mouth; it tastes like Kool-Aid for grownups. I replace the glass in exactly the same sticky circle where I found it, with the lipstick marks turned toward Nana's chair.

I step into the dining room. The big Hoover vacuum is in the corner next to the credenza. It always reminds me of Nana's story about my Aunt Nancy, who died from a kidney infection when she was my age. Nana told me she was so sad after Nancy died that she would scream out her name when she vacuumed. She thought no one would hear her screaming when the vacuum was going. Then one day Nancy walked into the dining room from the kitchen and stood there in the doorway looking at Nana until she turned the vacuum off. She said, "Mother, I am fine. I want you to stop calling my name now." Nancy walked back into the kitchen. Nana ran after her, but she was gone, and the kitchen was empty. She said she stopped calling Nancy. She was glad she was okay, but she still missed her.

I look at the spot where Nana said Nancy had been and wonder what she looked like. Nana never called her a ghost. She just said she was Nancy.

I run to stand in the kitchen door and wait for Nana to turn around. She smiles and comes over to me. She sings, "Good morning, merry sunshine. How did you wake so soon? You scared the little stars away and shined away the moon." I know it is a song for babies, but Nana loves it. Then she says, "Good morning, Virginia." That's my mother's name. But I don't care. Nana doesn't remember names very well. I just like the way she looks at me when she says it.

This is the moment when I stand and open myself to pure love—love that I can completely depend upon.

I go right to the green bread box. Yes! A full package of Bay's English muffins. Back at home, with six siblings, I get only my share. Here, I can have the whole package if I want.

I walk past Nana, over to the fridge, and I yank it open. Right at eye level there are pigs' feet in a large jar. I don't like to look at the little hooves or the place where the foot was cut off. Worst of all are thick black hairs that sprout randomly all over the feet. This is my grandfather's favourite snack. He loves pigs' feet, and I love him in spite of that.

On the bottom shelf is a full carton of six bottles of Hires root beer, on its side. I clap my hands twice with pleasure. The door to the little freezer scrapes and creaks against encrusted ice as I coax it open. I imagine it's what Frosty the Snowman's asshole looks like. Inside is a pint of Borden's vanilla ice cream, with the cheerful picture of Elsie, the Borden cow, grinning at me. And her husband, Elmer. There is plenty to make root beer floats. Black cows, Nana calls them. I will get one after lunch and another after dinner. I close the refrigerator door carefully, jiggling the handle just so to make it stay shut, glancing at Nana to get her smile of approval.

I come to the table and sit, watching my grandfather in a Dago t-shirt, his middle-aged man breasts jiggling slightly when he moves. He is unshaven, grizzly and jowly, smelling of sweat and stale cigars. I love his smell.

I love watching how he eats his breakfast the same way every day. His big, deep white bowl holds half a muskmelon, giving off that familiar strong, sweet summer smell. After he finishes the melon, he dumps the rind in the garbage and refills the bowl with cornflakes, sugar and milk. When he finishes the cereal, he fills the bowl with coffee. The whole meal from just one bowl. I think this is so clever. Even now, I consider this a basic life skill and try to do the same thing today, except that muskmelon does not exist in British Columbia.

Without being reminded, I go to the bathroom to wash my hands before eating. Cashmere Bouquet soap is at the sink, but I use the green bar of Palmolive from the tub. I feel uncomfortable using Cashmere Bouquet because that was what we usually gave to the nuns for Christmas presents. I cannot use it without feeling a strange sense of shame. Thankfully, I don't feel that way now.

I skip back to the kitchen and toast two muffins. The butter is on the counter, already softening in the summer heat. I practically ladle it onto the muffins. Some always drips down my chin onto my t-shirt. At home, we only have butter on holidays.

After breakfast I run down the back stairs and out into the yard. I climb the catalpa tree, collect the long, pointed beans and throw them down into a pile. Later I stack them behind the garage for use as weapons in case there is another war coming.

Nana calls me in and sends me to get cigarettes. I set out through the weeds of the vacant lot next door with thirty-five cents in my left hand and a stick in my right, which I flail in front of me to break the banana spider webs that appeared overnight. Afforded safe passage in this way, I head to the little diner that faces onto Hohman Avenue.

Arriving at the cigarette machine, I push the quarter and dime into the slot, listening to be sure they drop into place. I grasp the metal handle beneath the Pall Malls firmly with both hands. I plant my feet next to the machine, lean back, take a deep breath and pull with great resolve. One, then two clanks come from deep inside the machine. A package of Pall Malls drops into the tray. Three pennies—change for the cigarettes—are taped to the pack. Those three pennies are mine.

Outside the diner I carefully remove the tape and stick the pennies in my pocket. I begin to plan my penny-candy shopping. Coconut in the shape and general colour of watermelon slices. Pink buttons on a strip of paper. A small Tootsie Roll. No, instead of the Tootsie Roll, I will get Mary Janes. They come two in a package for only a penny and last a long time. I won't spend the pennies until I get near home, where the penny-candy store is. I feel a deep sense of satisfaction with my plans for a wise and thrifty purchase.

I look at the cigarettes as I head home on the web-free path. On the front of the package it says, "Where distinguished people congregate." I feel proud of my grandmother for smoking special cigarettes. I break into a trot as I approach the house. I wonder whether the milkman has come yet and whether he will leave some chocolate milk. I am eager to present the cigarettes to my grandmother; she will hug and kiss me when I do.

That feeling of being cherished has stayed with me my entire life. I wish every child could have access to such love and every adult could have such memories.

We don't all have grandmothers like Nana. Many of us have to find or create or perhaps simply imagine such loving figures. My hope is that in reading this, you are reminded of times when love suffused you and took over your cells. Or maybe simply reading this story will help do that for you.

A Nun's Hug

All my life I have been carried on the shoulders of others.

I was a little afraid of Sister Frieda. A no-nonsense nun, she was not only the principal of Our Lady of Grace School but also the teacher of forty-four Grade 6 students. She leaned over my desk, smelling like Cashmere Bouquet soap, all black robes and that white thing framing her face. Thick glasses made her eyes look goggly. There were strange black dots on her nose. They were just enlarged pores, but they were strange to me. Her breath was different. Not bad breath, exactly, just different. Like the smell of someone else's house is different.

Sister Frieda entered me into the spelling bee sponsored by the *Hammond Times*, our local newspaper. I would never have done that on my own; I was far too shy. I finished second—I spelled *picknicking* rather than *picnicking*—and was devastated because I had failed my school, my classmates and especially

Sister Frieda. It made no difference that I was awarded a Benrus watch.

On the way home afterward, my dad took the car down a different street and I asked where we were going. "We're going to the convent to report to Sister Frieda, honey." I did not want to do that because of my shame.

Until then, I had not realized there was such a thing as a convent. I had assumed the nuns were kept in a kind of storage area and brought out to teach us every morning. (Actually, this was not so far from the truth.)

We entered the foyer. It had a couple of chairs and a large crucifix and a statue of Our Lady of Grace. Sister Frieda appeared and raised a questioning eyebrow. My mother said, "He is sad because he finished second, Sister." I burst into tears. Sister Frieda looked at me, threw back her head and burst into laughter. She rushed across the room toward me, black robes all wild like the Wicked Witch, and gave me a big hug. I was shocked to feel a body under that nun's habit; my first thought was that I was going to go to hell for having contact with a nun's body. In that most un-nun-like moment, in that spontaneous hug, with her joyful laughter in response to my self-inflicted judgment of failure, she showed she had faith in me. She held that faith for me long before I had faith in myself.

She remains in my memory as having extraordinary beauty and helping to build that beauty in me.

A Roche Family Christmas

It was Christmas Eve 1961. From the front window of our house on Ridge Road, looking to the north and Lake Michigan, we saw the pink glow of the eternal dawn created by the blast furnaces and slag dumps of the steel mills of Gary, Indiana. Our version of the Christmas star. The wind swept snow and bitter cold down off the lake, whipping the bare branches of the oak trees in the yard. There were no beautiful snowdrifts in our corner of northwest Indiana. Instead, jagged grey ice formations decorated the landscape. Constant pollution from the mills and refineries meant we never used the words *crisp* or *crystalline* to describe our winters.

Inside, it was warm. There was Mom, Dad, me, Craig, Kathleen, Patrick, Kevin, Michael and Teresa. Yes, Irish Catholics. All seven kids were in our pyjamas, fresh out of the shower.

We stood around the dining room table, the centre of our family life. Big enough to seat all nine of us, it ordinarily was covered with a bright, floral-patterned oilcloth. For this special night, my mother had purchased a new white plastic Christmas tablecloth from the Ben Franklin Five and Ten Cent Store in downtown Highland. Printed with green and red poinsettias, reindeer, wreaths, candles and snowmen, it displayed all the symbols of a secular Christmas that we couldn't escape, even as Catholics.

In the centre of the table was a chrome-plated metal tray with six matching metal wine glasses. Why metal? These were not heirlooms. They were not wedding gifts. I don't recall where they came from. The point is, they were durable. The design slogan was "form follows durability." At least they were not cast iron. Martha Stewart would have lasted two or three minutes in our house before bolting.

Those special glasses always and only appeared on Christmas Eve, as did the accompanying bottle of Mogen David Concord-grape wine. In the US Midwest back then, our wine choices were limited. Wine was usually sold from the shelves above and behind bartenders in the taverns outside the steel mills. Richard's Wild Irish Rose was the most popular. It was bright red, the colour of hair tonic or Kool-Aid. Then there were the varietals: Thunderbird, Ripple and the awful stuff that the priests drank at Mass—one would think it would have deterred them from alcoholism. In those times, Mogen David was actually the sophisticated choice. During the rest of the year, our family's sacramental beverage was Stroh's Fire-Brewed Beer.

My father poured the syrupy stuff. Each of us had about three ounces (including Teresa, the youngest at six years old), except for Patrick, who requested and received Royal Crown Cola served in a shot glass. Dietary quirks were prevalent and tolerated in our family, usually because it meant that the rest of us got a larger share of whatever was being served. In this case, Pat's preference for RC Cola meant the other six of us each got one of the metal wineglasses. My parents used special Welch's grape jelly Christmas edition glasses. We drank a toast to Christmas and to Jesus's birthday.

Fortified and filled with tiddly Christmas spirit, we cheerfully organized ourselves into a procession. There was little scuffling or jostling for position, thanks to Mogen David and to the ostensible solemnity of the occasion. We knew the drill and marched out the door of the dining room in order by age. Our destination: the nativity scene in the living room. Teresa was first. In her hands she cradled little Baby Jesus in his manger; her job was to place him in the centre of the tableau.

Our creche had also been purchased from the Ben Franklin. Our house never contained any carved wood or porcelain or anything at all dainty. Our manger scene had to be one that could take significant abuse. Jesus, Mary, Joseph, two angels, the donkey, the oxen, the lambs and the three Wise Men (two white, one black) all frequently crashed to the floor. Whenever that happened, we accused the offender of having committed a mortal sin and then reverently reconstructed the scene.

Our Baby Jesus was a crudely moulded piece of plastic, already permanently embedded into his manger. All you could see of Jesus was his face (white with blue eyes) and hair (bright yellow). The rest was covered with plastic swaddling. The general impression was of an ice-cream cone. His eyes had been stamped on by some machine in Japan and were askew. The left eye was higher than the right and gazed about ten degrees off centre. His little pink mouth had also been imprinted just a bit west of where it should have been. In our house, nobody talked about the fact that my face was disfigured. So I never revealed that I secretly loved the Baby Jesus whose face, I thought, looked a little bit like mine.

We marched out through the front hall, Teresa holding Jesus, the rest of us with lit candles, all singing "Silent Night." Singing was not highly valued in our family. Catholics do not sing much now, and we sang even less back then. We were all off key. Not off key together, but each of us off key in our own way.

The pilgrimage into the living room took about a minute, which was good because none of us knew the second verse of "Silent Night." Teresa placed plastic Jesus in the centre of the manger scene so we could all gaze upon him and he upon us (with his right eye). We took our seats, grateful that we had finished our yearly songfest and pilgrimage.

The next part of our ritual was the drawing of lots— little folded pieces of paper with the numbers one through seven—to see who would get first choice of a location on which to put their presents in the morning. Most coveted were the chairs that did not have to be shared with a sibling. In a family with seven children, much of our time was devoted to lower-level primate activities such as establishment of boundaries and territory.

Then it was time for my father to bless the Christmas tree. He read from a book, *Blessings for All Occasions*, which we had purchased after Mass on Sunday from the ladies in the back of the church. It contained, for example, "Blessing for a New Car," "Blessing for a Fishing Trip," "Blessing for a Sprained Ankle." It was a typical Catholic publication. Random, uncontrolled blessing was not encouraged. As my father read, he sprinkled the tree with holy water stolen from the church font.

Dad had an embarrassed smile on his face. He was not used to being in a position of honoured authority in the family. Mom was our driving force on occasions like these. She was the one who made sure our rituals happened. We knew we would all be going to Mass and Communion together in the morning. Then Dad really started getting into it. There was plenty of holy water left, so he decided to bless all of us. He sprinkled away and began improvising in Latin, repeating random phrases from Mass. *Dominus vobiscum. Kyrie eleison. Credo in unum Deum.* Partly it was the effect of the Mogen David, but mostly he just appreciated having an audience.

A special event had been scheduled for this particular Christmas Eve. Little Teresa had learned a new song in school: "The Huron Christmas Carol." She was going to sing a solo for us. My father introduced her, but somehow, with the wine, *huron* came out as *urine*. "The Urine Christmas Carol!" What a wonderful Christmas gift this mispronunciation was for us. A Christmas miracle! We all giggled softly, trying to suppress our mirth and not spoil Teresa's moment.

Teresa began singing angelically—a surprise to our off-key family. Our great-aunt Rose beamed from the easy chair. Too arthritic for the procession, she had waited as a special guest. She was a pink-cheeked matriarch, but inside she was a warrior, a strong and feisty old woman. Rose MacFarlane was born in the 1880s. During the entire twentieth century, she had warred against the constant, inexorable undermining and destruction of all the values she had held dear. As she approached eighty, her feistiness was turning to obdurate crankiness. Here tonight, on Christmas Eve, she was in her glory. It was the birthday of Jesus, the family was together, and little Teresa was singing "The Urine Christmas Carol." Aunt

Rose began to weep with joy. It was too much for the rest of us. Our suppressed giggling turned into chortles and snorts.

Aunt Rose looked around. Here, before her eyes, was more evidence that everything she valued was crumbling. She once again found herself surrounded by mocking heretics. Her euphoria turned into rage. She reached down, grabbed her heavy wooden cane and swung it in an arc. Because of her arthritis, the cane moved very slowly. At first, we did not realize what was happening. Then we saw that she intended to whack my brother Kevin, who had the misfortune to be the one within range.

No one intervened. Our laughter increased. As did Kevin's. It was like watching The Three Stooges in slow motion, with Aunt Rose as Moe. The cane ascended, shaking, but driven by enormous willpower and righteous anger. As it rose to its zenith, our laughter also crescendoed. The cane headed downward of its own momentum. Kevin did not try to escape. Like a good Catholic, he accepted his punishment—with exceptional good humour. *Crack!* The cane fell across his shins. Kevin moaned and toppled from the chair, tears spurting from his eyes. He writhed in pain but never stopped laughing.

Captured in that moment was the essence of a Roche family Christmas.

Postscript

I emailed this story to my siblings and they mostly agreed with the details. Teresa, however, did not believe we had been laughing at "The Urine Christmas Carol." For the many years since then, she had been carrying the memory that we had been laughing at her singing. It took some time to convince her otherwise, but we did.

No Bashful Need Apply

At the unemployment office on 16th Street, I found a notice on the bulletin board: "Manufacturer of adult products. No bashful need apply." I had recently arrived in San Francisco from Indiana, where I had been a computer programmer, a job I hated. I wanted to work with people. I didn't realize what that might mean in San Francisco.

It's true that I was somewhat bashful. But the ad did not say I *should* not apply, it just said I did not *need* to apply. I decided to go for it.

Pen-Vib, Inc. was located in a flat on 17th Street, right across from Sanchez Elementary School. From the outside, there was no indication that this was where adult products were manufactured. When I stepped inside, the only thing that struck me was a pervasive plasticky aroma.

Julia, the owner, met me at the door. I was a little surprised to find that the manufacturer of adult products was a well-dressed, middle-aged woman. After the usual job-interview-type questions, she asked me what my sign was.

Luckily, I was aware that I was a Capricorn. I didn't know what that meant, but it obviously was important to Julia. She hired me on the spot. I was the only man among the thirteen applicants.

Julia explained that Pen-Vib manufactured dildos. I nodded. I understood the concept of a dildo but had never met one face to face.

My duties were ludicrously simple. I came in at 9:00 a.m., opened the mail, paid the bills, balanced the chequing account, did some filing. The most important things I did were to tidy up the office a bit and arrange Julia's mail and messages in an orderly way on her desk. This created the illusion of competence for Julia, who lived in the chaos zone. She would come in around 11:00, go through the nice neat piles on her desk, make a couple of phone calls and leave for the racetrack with the wonderful illusion that things were under control.

Julia's son Russell came in once a week to do packing and shipping. For the actual dildo production, the go-to person was Annie, an older, stocky woman with a moustache who lived in the flat upstairs. She made the dildos in exchange for her rent. Annie would arrive at work early, scoop flesh-coloured chips out of a barrel and begin cooking up a pot of dildo on the kitchen stove. It was the same kind of plasticky material used to make artificial legs, arms, noses and other prosthetic devices, which made sense to me.

Flesh-coloured, of course, meant a pink colour similar to that of Bazooka bubble gum. This was in the 1970s when there was only one colour of dildo available. In our enlightened twenty-first century, dildos come in as many colours as Baskin-Robbins flavours. But this was still the neodildoic age.

By the time I got there, the place was filled with the smell of hot dildo, which was what I had noticed on that first day. Annie sang Baptist hymns while she stirred the dildo soup. "He took my, he took my, he took my sins away." "Oh, he walks with me and he talks with me and he tells me I am his own ..." Then she would carefully pour the hot dildo-to-be soup into moulds.

As she sang and stirred and poured, I sat in the front office watching the Sanchez students flood onto the blacktop playground, shrilling and chirping, running and jumping during their morning recess. I enjoyed both Annie's hymns and my own delicious sense of dissociation. Annie didn't talk much. I don't think she enjoyed her job. I doubt she described her sense of dissociation as delicious. When I told her I enjoyed her singing, she merely harrumphed.

When I was alone, I looked through the shelves in the shipping room where the dildo stock was stored. Wow! Some of these things were not sex toys—they were more like lifestyles. The smaller sizes looked like doggie bones next to the XXLS, which had enough heft and size to be slung over my shoulder. The varieties! There were strange bumps, and even one that seemed to have venereal warts. Weird appendages protruded at strange angles. When I accidentally turned on the vibrator in one of the big guys, I jumped a foot in the air and practically fainted. Welcome to San Francisco and "working with people."

Pen-Vib distributed other products. A popular seller was the Jac-U-Lator penis enlarger, a powerful manually operated vacuum pump that I would never in a million years let near my penis. Well, a million years is an exaggeration. Two days was more accurate. It worked! I was afraid I would explode and not sure whether I could get workers' comp if that happened, so I put it back in the box and returned it to the shelf.

I also browsed through the files while Julia was at the track. Brochures and samples of all varieties introduced me to a vast array of pornography. I was amazed by the panoply of activities displayed. Another chapter in the delayed sex education of a good Irish Catholic boy.

After a few weeks of snooping file by file (in the interest of research, of course), I got to the back of the bottom file drawer and a folder full of letters to Pen-Vib. The first thing that struck me as unusual was how matter of fact the customers were about their proclivities and practices. It was so different from the world I'd grown up in, where even the thought of, say, a nipple was enough to condemn you to an eternity in hell covered with flaming boils. Unless you got to confession first. Anything sexual, whether physical or imaginary, was drenched with shame.

Then I found many letters from people with disabilities. Special orders and thank yous from people with varying physical conditions, for whom sexual aids were as necessary as crutches or glasses or hearing aids. Some requested custom work that included creative suggestions about improving the products, such as variable-speed vibrators. A letter from a woman in Kansas, a widow, who knew that God understood her using her vibrator because her Methodist minister had told her so. These writers did not seem like strange people at all. I can see now that they were on the leading edge of safe-sex practices.

Suddenly this world was not as kinky as it had seemed when I first started working there. I wouldn't say Pen-Vib was epiphanous for me, but it was definitely revelatory. It was there that I had my first contact with the disabled community. And it was an introduction to the possibility of shame-free sexuality. What a novel concept! I was no longer quite so bashful.

Camping with Amy

Bouncing around in the back of Terry Katz's old Ford van, I held tight to my five-year-old daughter, Amy. Next to us was Terry's partner, Naomi, with their five-year-old son, Dmitri, on her lap. Terry rocked and reared the van over and around boulders as he searched for a certain lake he'd told us he remembered from his childhood. It was 1973. We were at almost sixty-five hundred feet in California's Sierra Nevada, and I was about to be introduced to the joys of camping.

I was dubious. Not only had I no camping experience, I had very little vacation experience. I'd grown up in a big, working-class family and our vacation trips were mostly at Lake Michigan's Miller Beach, about half an hour from where we lived.

When I was six years old, in 1950, my beloved grandparents took me on a thousand-mile road trip from Chicago to Denver. Many scenes from that trip are embedded in my memory and in my cells, particularly the sight of the Rocky Mountains drawing nearer and nearer as we drove west. The rivers of my childhood were muddy, slow moving and polluted; bullheads, carp and catfish were the only fish that could survive. But the Rocky Mountain streams were clear and drinkable, a fast-moving delight. I had reached into a narrow stream channel and scooped out a small trout with my bare hands. The memory of that trip overcame any doubts about what we were doing and where we were heading in Terry's van.

Terry veered onto a quasi-road strewn with white granite and found the spot he had remembered, near a little nameless snowmelt lake. This was unfamiliar territory to someone like me, raised around the steel mills and oil refineries of north-west Indiana. The Sierra Buttes were etched against the sky. I did double takes, staring at them, assimilating their being, trying to grasp in reality what I had only seen in paintings or photographs or films.

I had never slept outside before except for a few summer nights in the backyard in tents made of blankets that absorbed the dew in the early morning and gave off the scent of humans accumulated over the years. Here, the air seemed almost edible. The firs, the mountain misery (a fragrant evergreen shrub native to California) that grew underfoot everywhere, the deer brush in blossom—all the aromas of early summer in the mountains intoxicated me.

We arrived just before nightfall and threw our tarps and sleeping bags onto the flattest spots we could find after clearing away branches and pine cones. There was no time to find firewood. The sudden night chill made me eager to get Amy settled and myself into my own sleeping bag. I had never spent the night in a sleeping bag, and we did not even have tents to shelter us. The kids chatted for a while, then slipped into sleep, as I did soon after. That first night in the wild was a restless one. At one point I rolled over, thinking someone was shining a flashlight in my face. Instead a glorious full moon was rising, whose reflection in the lake doubled the light.

Later, after moonset, I came half awake again to the sound of lurching and thrashing nearby. Shards of a monster paradigm exploded in my reptilian brain: *Sounds like … sounds big, brown or grey-green, rank smell, sharp body parts, bad! … flesh ripping, slobbery mouth … a bear coming toward us? Am I soon to die?* Then the mammalian brain, the cerebellum, kicked in, and no, the thing was only making purposeless motions in the alder thicket down by the lake, with no progress toward my sleeping bag. No death. Safe. (*Stupid monster, stupid.*)

Terry was also awake. He whispered, "It's a deer." A deer! A deer? Like Bambi? Who bounded noiselessly through the dappled forest? Bambi did not make thudding, thumping noises when he ran, or crash through the thickets like a creature from a B-grade horror movie.

In the morning, the kids woke in a frenzy of excitement and headed down to the lake. I stayed in the sleeping bag until the sun hit me, exulting in the aroma of pancakes from the cast-iron frying pan.

We stayed a week, and I was enchanted. I immediately started planning to come back the next year, for the whole summer, just me, Amy and Blue, our friend Gary's German Shepherd. My friends thought I had too little experience in the woods to do this, and that Amy was too young, and of course they were absolutely right. But she and I had both become addicted.

All through the next winter, I saved carefully. Very carefully. I was more or less a hippie at this time, working at the Childcare Switchboard and Single Parent Resource Center of San Francisco for $300 a month. I was living rent-free in the parsonage of Bethany Methodist Church with three other men. We were trying to revitalize a dying parish and remake it into a community-oriented church.

I carefully watched the advertisements in the sports pages for camping equipment. I wandered through the Army & Navy store on Market Street with Amy in tow. We bought tube tents, an inflatable boat, a propane stove, a trench tool. The luxury purchase was a Zebco Pocket Fisherman, the kind I had seen on late-night TV commercials.

I planned out our menu for the entire summer and filled the roof rack on our sky-blue VW Bug with everything we would need to eat. I scavenged empty plastic gallon mayonnaise jars from restaurants, washed them, and filled them with pinto beans, cornmeal, rice and pancake mix. I took a three-month leave of absence from my job at the Childcare Switchboard.

Amy and I and Blue drove up to a higher elevation than the previous summer and found a primitive campsite, a slight clearing among the pines at about seven thousand feet. The earth beneath was spongy with castoff pine needles. About twenty-five feet away, a snowmelt stream flowed the entire summer. We discovered an old wooden cabinet nailed to a tree close by a fire ring. It had gnaw marks on the outside but no animal had gotten in, so we had a ready-made pantry.

Next to the campsite was a mountain meadow, which at the time we arrived had not yet burst into bloom. Patches of snow remained in places that hid from the June sun. During the course of the summer, we watched the whole life cycle of that meadow. Before our eyes, plants emerged from dry ground overnight, grew, budded, bloomed, faded and were replaced with eager new growth. The meadow lived, died, lived, died.

We settled in. It took a few days, and we had to acclimate to mountain life. Amy had spent her life walking on concrete and asphalt, so she stumbled for a while on the slanted and rocky ground. For the first week or so, we went hatless as we hiked around and then wondered why we felt disoriented, cranky and slightly nauseous in the evening. When we caught on to the reality of sun stroke, we always wore our caps and kerchiefs.

Blue the dog was much more immediately at home. His marmot addiction came into full flower. From their hiding places in the boulder piles, the rodents taunted him with beautiful piercing whistles. Blue, powerless to resist, charged out of the campsite, leaping from boulder to boulder till he found their hiding place. He barked to notify us of his success, then stuck his snout into the darkness. He bottomed out in his addiction when he got a nose and attitude adjustment from a marmot incisor.

For some reason, the beans and rice—our staples—would not cook. They boiled for hours yet remained inedibly hard. I mentioned this puzzling fact to the woman behind the counter at Bassett's Station, the store a few miles down the mountain. She laughed and explained how water boiled at a lower temperature at higher elevations. So it was mostly pancakes and cookies for the rest of the summer, and that turned out to be just fine. You get used to that sort of thing—and more—while camping.

Just as vegetation came and went, so did insect life. Around the Fourth of July, inch-long squirmy green worms began dropping out of the trees. They landed on our clothes, our heads, our sleeping bags. For a few days we tried brushing them off. It was useless. I even got tired of picking them out of the pancake batter—the extra protein was a sort of manna. I think Amy's complaints about a wormy taste were mostly imagined, especially when they were doused with Aunt Jemima.

Our lives were so simple. We ate. We walked around. We ate again. We sat for a while. Wandered around again. Ate. Sat around the fire until it died down. We slept. In the morning we stayed in the sleeping bags until the sun hit and took away the early-morning chill. Then we crawled out. I fixed breakfast. Many days we did not go farther than a few hundred feet from the campsite.

Amy's friend Dmitri came to stay with us for a week. One morning I awoke to the sound of him and Amy squealing like the marmots. Four inches of snow had fallen during the night of the summer solstice. We packed our essentials into the vw and headed downslope to a motel in Sierraville. I was upset, concerned about the cost of the motel and the possible loss of our stuff to the melting snow. I brooded on the motel bed. I noticed that Amy and Dmitri were talking behind the bathroom door. They danced out into the bedroom and started twirling around me, waving their arms, laughing and chanting, "Relax. Relaax. *Relaaax.*" The snow was completely gone by the next day and the temperature was in the eighties.

Several times, drenching thunderstorms came out of nowhere. We huddled in our tents. Another time, a huge old tree fell nearby just at daybreak, popping us a couple of inches into the air as it smashed into the ground.

Most all the time, it was a wonderful dream time for Amy and me.

We waded up the streams through the clear and fragrant water. We clambered over boulders and logs, collecting centuries-rounded rocks. Still pools mesmerized us, with salamanders and trout and fool's gold glistening at the bottom, insects dancing and glimmering across the surface.

Coming around a stream's bend, we found mountain azaleas in full white bloom, arching across the water like fragrant foam, luring butterflies that flitted all about.

I always hiked with my wildflower book in the day pack. Amy's job was to find the flowers. One time she spied the single bloom of a bright-orange Washington lily about a quarter of a mile downstream. She yelled for me to stop and she pointed it out. I could not see it through the foliage, but I trusted her. She had sharp eyes and delighted in the beauty around her. So we picked our way downstream and found it.

My job was to look up and identify the flowers. I can remember that Washington lily, exactly where it was and what it looked like. I can tell you where to find the spice bush at Oregon Creek, the scarlet penstemon in the boulders above Packer Lake and the dark places where the woodland pinedrops emerge from the forest floor. It was especially wonderful to find things that were edible, like the gooseberries and the wild onion that grew not far from our campsite (delicious with green worms!).

After lunch I would lean back against a tree in the shade and doze as I listened to the stream burbling. Pine cones popped open in the heat of the day. Steller's jays squawked at any hint of movement, squirrels chattered and Blue whoofed up dust as he napped and dreamed in the semi-shade close by. Amy, always lured by water, played down by the stream.

We sometimes drove down the mountainside to Sand Pond. Its sandy bottom had been formed by mine tailings left many years previously and it was warmer than the many alpine lakes in the area. The first time we went there, it was early morning and much too cold to swim. Instead, we paddled across in our inflatable boat. At the far shore, we came to an exquisite yellow pond lily. I reached out of the boat, picked it and never saw another pond lily for thirty-five years.

I watched Amy swimming with other children, listened to their shouts as they jumped into the water, with the wind soughing through the surrounding pines. The Sierra Buttes loomed overhead, bare and rocky except for a few northern snowy crevices.

What a glorious summer. To have spent it in the company of my six-year-old daughter was a gift beyond compare. We cemented a father-daughter bond that has endured since, even through difficult times.

Standing at the Back Door of Happiness, Part 1

The Communist Years

For me, happiness had always stood somewhere off-stage. For many years, I struggled with answering the question, "Are you happy?" with a simple yes. The best I could do was list all the reasons why I should be happy, consider the list and agree that I probably was happy.

Here is the core lesson about happiness that I learned from the Baltimore Catechism. I still know it by heart:

Q: "Why did God make you?"

A: "God made me to know, love, and serve Him in this world, and to be happy with Him forever in heaven."

As I approached my thirties, it seemed I was not to have any illusions about being happy in this lifetime. I had never dealt with my facial difference. I mostly lived in the vale of tears. I concentrated on being a good boy who did what he was told. I (almost) always tried to be responsible and to change the world.

In 1972, I co-founded the Childcare Switchboard and

Single Parent Resource Center of San Francisco. We were hippies who wanted to bring co-operative childcare to San Francisco. Instead, open phone lines let us hear from parents, many of them single, who needed childcare and other services simply to survive and keep their families together. I listened to them and learned the truth about being a parent in my city, and what I heard angered me—especially the disparity between the mouthings of politicians and the reality of being a single parent, particularly one on AFDC (Aid to Families with Dependent Children).

I was part of a successful effort to pass a ballot resolution stating that the provision of childcare to all was the official policy of the City of San Francisco. Unfortunately, it was not legally binding. The response of the city government was to form the Mayor's Committee on Childcare, and I was a member. I soon found out that it was composed of people more interested in getting money for themselves ("we need more studies") than in providing needed services. I left, disgusted by liberal politics.

I had friends who were joining left-wing political organizations. I was impressed by their dedication and finally became convinced that, if I were honest with myself, there simply was no other way to accomplish change. I decided to become a committed communist.

After a seriously Catholic childhood, which included four years (age thirteen through seventeen) in a seminary studying to be a priest, I was to spend twelve years in the Democratic Workers Party. It was a fairly seamless transition from Catholicism: infallible leaders, confession/criticism and self-criticism, paradise/dictatorship of the proletariat as the carrot—all were familiar to me. As was an emphasis on work and responsibility.

The Democratic Workers Party was founded by a group of ten women led by Marlene Dixon. I thought this meant it would be different from the many leftist/Trotskyist/Maoist/ etc. organizations that were proliferating at the time. And indeed it was, but not always in the ways I had hoped.

The party was a culture in which the only promised reward was implicit in our slogan "work hard, play hard." The commitment demanded that you be a person who could rebuild the party from scratch if everyone else was killed. For me, membership was like being at a protest march you did not really want to be attending, carrying a sign that symbolized and carried the weight of nonexistent commitment. "Play hard," which masqueraded as encouragement, actually meant "get drunk" like a slobbering animal.

To all appearances I was a true believer, but as years went by, belief receded into the background and sheer willpower took its place. Like my childhood belief in the virgin birth, it was the right and responsible thing to believe in. And to do.

I was a full-time cadre in the Democratic Workers Party, devoted to the cause, averaging five to six hours of sleep a night and working during all waking hours. Ironically, I had decided to join the party because of what I had learned working at the Switchboard. I was an activist motivated not by ideology but by a desire to be of help to the mothers we heard from daily.

By 1982 I had been a party member for eight years. For the first five of these, I had grown personally. I had learned to challenge myself to do things I'd never done before, such as speaking in public (although I was kept on a tight leash due to my untrustworthy sense of humour). I had several lovers along the way (although love never trumped discipline). The party became a successful part of the political landscape in the San Francisco Bay area, mainly through our front organizations the Rebel Worker Organization (RWO) and the Grass Roots Alliance (GRA), both of which reflected the diversity of San Francisco. Through the GRA, we organized successfully in every neighbourhood in San Francisco, from the Tenderloin to Chinatown to the Mission barrio to the already dwindling African American areas in Bayview-Hunters Point and the Western Addition, and throughout the minority and working-class neighbourhoods in Oakland. In 1979 we came within a couple of percentage points of passing the Tax the Corporations initiative in San Francisco. Criticism/self-criticism still functioned, at least in part, as a way to sustain our common values. For me, those values were the sense of community and dedication to service.

Around the world, socialism had seemed to be pushing above the horizon. But as the passion of the 1960s and early 1970s wore down, the party became gradually more corrupt, cultlike and corroded by rampant alcoholism. The founder, Marlene Dixon, formerly a brilliant teacher, began functioning, unbeknownst to those of us in the rank and file, in an alcoholic haze. As happens in most cults, an inner circle protected her and assumed rigid control. At the lower levels, control mechanisms became more pronounced.

Criticism and self-criticism, instead of being a way of holding one another accountable to common values, began serving as a bullying tactic. We were sleep deprived and isolated from friends and family, if only by dint of the doctrinaire lives we led.

At one point I was ordered to attend a special meeting. As often happened, I wasn't told what it was about; I was just told to be there. In the meeting room, a dozen of us had been gathered. We were told to describe our conditions and then discuss what it meant to be an activist with chronic illness.

I had never considered myself to have chronic illness, and I was not sure why others thought I did. But I followed orders and told what had happened to me as an infant and child. As I spoke, I saw that my description of having multiple surgeries as a baby, of heavy radiation therapy that was ill measured and poorly targeted, of having gold pellets filled with radon gas imbedded along the left side of my face, of having a radiation burn on my eyelid, affected the others deeply. That was the first time I realized, though dimly, that I was highly symbolic. The exact nature of what my life was like on a day-to-day basis was not as important as what I looked like, not as important as the fact that I'd had radiation therapy. *Disability* and *illness* were not words I used to describe myself, they were words others used to describe their experience of me. I was a perfect example of the social model of disability.

I had grown up in the generation of denial. My parents and six siblings rarely talked about my facial difference. I did not even know my exact diagnosis until I was about thirty and certainly had never had the experience of describing my medical history to a group of others. I left the meeting wrestling with a newly acquired identity.

By this time, my colleagues at the Childcare Switchboard had nicknamed me "the Sleeper." I'd fall asleep at the phone station between incoming calls. On breaks, I'd slip back to the kitchen, to the toddler play area in the corner. I would curl myself into the little cavelike playhouse, draw the curtain and take a twenty-minute nap. Kids assumed I was part of the equipment and either ignored or clambered over me.

Near the end of the party, a crack appeared in the laboriously maintained façade, in the Potemkin village of discipline and commitment. I now believe that it was engendered in an alcoholic fog, in one of those half minutes of humanity that alcohol allows the alcoholic. A directive was issued to find out whether the cadres were "happy." I did not know what they were talking about or why they would ask such a question. I was simply unable to give the correct answer. I said, "I am productive. Does that count?"

That was my understanding of happiness. I could always generate some amount of self-satisfaction for doing what I thought I was supposed to be doing to save the world. Meanwhile, I slipped further into a depressed state. I was not able to gain access to my own soul.

The Bus Story

The prospect of standing up and giving a speech on a San Francisco Muni bus was disconcerting. I had been given orders to do it. All of us in the Democratic Workers Party had received those orders, but a week had passed, and no one had done anything. We were heavily involved in trying to defeat Proposition 13, the Jarvis-Gann Amendment, at the polls. We knew the people we wanted to reach were the ones who rode buses. I did want to obey orders, but something deeper and more important to me was at stake.

Around 8:30 a.m., still in the time window for school and work travel, I stood at the corner of 24th and Mission Streets in San Francisco. People dressed for work downtown stepped briskly onto the BART station's down escalator and slid out of sight. Most of them had come down the hill from the Noe

Valley neighbourhood on the 48 Quintara and were headed to the financial district or Civic Center.

Seated on the low wall around the plaza were shabbier folks, those who perhaps had been up all night, who needed morning sun to warm their bones, who needed human contact, who needed money for coffee and an Egg McMuffin from across the street. Among them were those from Central American villages, where the plaza in the centre of their town was where their day began.

I had come to know the people of San Francisco well in my eight years of counselling work at the Childcare Switchboard and Single Parent Resource Center, and then even more in years of community organizing with the Grass Roots Alliance. I knew that many of them would be on the #14 bus I was about to board: perhaps a Latina from Vera Cruz, four and a half feet tall, occupying one third of a double seat; men and women just getting off janitorial shifts; people with arthritis, high blood pressure and diabetes headed for Monteagle Medical Center and Saint Luke's Hospital; men wearing San Francisco Giants caps and clothes that reeked of paint; seniors wearing their warmest coat, the one they had worn since the 1950s that sheltered their aging body from the San Francisco fog. These were the people with whom I had spoken one-on-one on the street, fine people, most always courteous even when they did not agree or did not wish to be disturbed or did not speak English. In the far back of the bus, a few teens were slouching, punching each other in the arm and laughing loudly.

I was no longer afraid of the ordinary people of San Francisco; I had grown from my contact with them. In an entirely unexpected way, I had rediscovered a spark of faith, particularly among the women, who had a living faith. I knew that Aurora, a staunch Catholic, just as staunchly an organizer, prayed quietly at Mass, and when I saw her with others discussing the closing of their clinic, she listened quietly, her head tilted toward the person she was in conversation with, almost as if she was praying then too. Willie Lee, Esther, Dorothy, Robert—they all were Baptists. Willie Lee, especially, spoke in blessings. They were always doing what they saw needed to be done. Their faith was a daily faith, an active faith, not rooted in dogma, but formed and nurtured in relationship and action.

I had been resolving to speak on the bus. More than a want, it had become an obsession. But on that day I did not have full faith in myself, and I moved forward carried by the faith I saw in others. My intention was to give a short speech on the bus about getting out the vote. I kept trying to remember what I wanted to say, but as I muttered under my breath, I could only get out two sentences and then I'd loop back to begin again, my brain on repeat.

Then my fare was in the box and I stood at the front of the bus, holding on as it swung into the traffic flow. I knew that the people in front of me on the bus were the neighbours and friends of Aurora and Esther, but in this crowd, suddenly they were different, harder for me to distinguish as individuals. They blurred together.

I began to speak but did not know what I was saying. I was aware that words were coming out of my mouth, but it was like listening to someone in another room through a closed door. I recognized some of my own words, I heard my cadence, I could tell that I was trying hard to say the words I had memorized, but I did not believe I was saying what I had intended.

I was much more conscious of the faces in front of me, some turning from the window, from conversations, books or newspapers, some up from a doze, all looking up at me with that look I am so familiar with, that look of struggling to assimilate and understand my disfigured face. I know now, when I see that look, that my spoken words will not be heard until my appearance has registered.

But I did not understand that then, on the bus. I tried to force myself away from focusing on stares. I heard myself stop speaking. I looked to my left at a young gentleman sitting up front. He was dressed in a coat and tie and had a briefcase on his lap. He looked me right in the eye.

I had a memory of an article that said if you speak to one person at a time, public speaking is not as scary. I thought from the man's appearance, from the way he was dressed, that he was middle class and white and would be polite and safe. I met his gaze and began again.

His mouth curled in contempt. He raised his briefcase half up from his lap and shook it at me. He screamed, "Get off the bus, you fucking deformed communist faggot," and he swung the briefcase at me.

This scene has lost all coherence; I cannot reconstruct it in my memory. All I have is bits and pieces, some as sharply etched as photos, others brief, slow-motion shots. I remember looking out the window and wishing I were on the sidewalk, but I don't even know whether that memory is accurate—maybe it's from another time on another bus. The man in the suit held his briefcase rigidly with two hands, squeezing it as he spoke loudly, partly castigating me, partly declaiming to other passengers, partly exhorting the driver to take action, mostly speaking to himself. My speaking out had unleashed his anger.

In front of me, the other passengers were still staring. I did not know how much time had passed. I did not know what I had said. I only knew that I had failed. I moved toward the back of the bus, wanting to sit by myself, making my way through a gauntlet of stares. I kept my eyes straight ahead, still sensing the curiosity of others who were encouraged to stare at me by my taking on a public persona. I was a supermodel on the runway.

I found a seat by myself and sat there in shame and misery.

A hand appeared in front of me, an older person's, a woman's hand. The skin was crepey and mottled. The hand shook. It was reaching for my hand. As it grasped mine, I looked up and into blue eyes that lit me up. She took my hand in both of hers and spoke in an Irish accent: "You did a fine job. A fine job." Then she turned toward the front of the bus and raised her voice. "You're the one who should be getting off the bus, you damned bully."

I sat stunned as she returned to her seat.

I felt another hand, from the seat behind, on my left shoulder, a large, brown, strong hand. Behind me were two young men, Latinos, wearing bandanas on their heads and plaid shirts buttoned up to the top button. Gang clothes. Gang members. Cholos. Now what?

The one with his hand on me said, "Homey! You know what?" And this time the accent was Central American.

"What?" I must have answered.

"You did a good job, man. A good job. But you know what?"

"No, what?"

"You got to get up and try it again."

With that, he stood, took my arm and shepherded me into the aisle. I stood there. People were still staring. Some were laughing at the scene. It was friendly laughter. One man motioned me toward the front of the bus.

My gang-member friend reached down, grabbed my belt from behind and hoisted me up and forward for a couple of steps. I got to the front of the bus. My heckler had left, and I gave my little speech more or less fully. At the end several people applauded. I felt flushed, not with success but with relief, and a bit of pride that I had actually done what I'd intended. I did not think to thank that old Irish lady or the young Latino guys. But I have never forgotten them and have carried gratitude for them in my heart for many years.

Standing at the
Back Door of Happiness,
Part 2

The Hard Road Out

By 1982, I still had not summoned the courage to leave the Democratic Workers Party. I kept doing what I thought I was supposed to do, should want to do, had to do to change the world.

From deep inside me, an escape plan appeared unbidden and fully formed. I knew where, when and how it would happen. At the Childcare Switchboard, I'd be sitting in the director's office, in a chair against the wall across from Helen's desk. I knew what I was going to do: stand, wobble, sag and topple over to my right. I knew that on the way down to the floor, I'd hit my head against the side of the plywood bookcase and that it would make an impressive and alarming sound without too much damage being done.

The plan stayed in my mind for a couple of weeks. I felt the possibility and lure of being unburdened of rules and responsibilities without having to express a conscious choice about it.

On the chosen day, I went home for lunch, already in an altered state, zombie-like, succumbing to an unknown force, focused on what I wanted to do, what was supposed to happen. I came back to the Switchboard, knocked on Helen's door, entered and sat in the chair as planned. She turned her chair around to face me. I looked at her heaping in-basket, at the piles of papers, and felt a flash of comfort at the thought of my leaving work behind. We started talking. Someone knocked at the door. Helen excused herself, went to answer the door and started a conversation, trying to meet the person's needs quickly so we could go on with our meeting. Time simultaneously slowed and quickened; I slipped above my physical self to watch my body deciding to stand. I rejoined my body and hesitated for a second, gathering my will without will. I slumped over just as I had visualized and let myself fall. My head thumped against the bookcase. I sagged to the floor. Helen turned and screamed, "David!"

The floor smelled dirty and dusty and safe, where I belonged. My body started shaking. That was not something I had chosen or planned. I began to gag and choke and spit up the lunch I had just eaten and the coffee I was drinking, and I wondered why that was happening. My plan had ended, and suddenly there was no plan, no more choices. I had given over control and could only observe. I loved the feeling of having no control, no more choices to be made, nothing on the to-do list. It felt blissful.

Co-workers gathered at the door. I did not look up at them. Helen shooed them away and covered me with a blanket. I heard talk out in the hall about an ambulance. I had not planned on an ambulance. I had not planned on anything past giving up. I wondered what was going to happen. I liked it there on the floor. I thought it would be fine to stay right there.

I heard paramedics coming up the stairs. A blond guy looked at me as if I was not myself but a bundle of symptoms. They did not talk to me; I don't even remember them reassuring me. They talked to Helen. I listened, hoping she would make sense out of the situation. "He collapsed. I think he has not been well for a while."

The feeling of being lifted and carried was soothing. I was strapped onto a gurney and pushed out into the hall. Swaying down the narrow stairway, I wanted just to relax and sleep; this was what I wanted, and I was happy to be safe in the gurney. The ambulance was waiting, right at the corner of 24th and Sanchez. I felt the heaviness of the vehicle as it eased off. I started at the sound of the siren, wondered whether I would fall out as we headed up the hill on Castro Street. But I was safe and relaxed until we got to Kaiser Hospital. Nothing bad could happen to me because there was nothing wrong with me. I was choosing to be disabled.

At Kaiser, the paramedics un-gurneyed me and placed me in a bed in a curtained-off space where I could listen to the sounds of the ER and wait my turn.

The smells of a hospital—the alcohol, the Betadyne, all came forward out of their waiting places. I began replicating what I had learned as an infant, toddler and child, when I had learned compliance, to be a good boy, to tolerate pain and discomfort, and to not cry.

I am a *fascinoma*. Physicians find me fascinating. I am unusual. They do not know what to do with me. I do not fit into a category, but that has never stopped them from trying to find one for me.

I withdrew inside myself, mentally, emotionally and spiritually, preparing for whatever was about to happen. I was in a bed surrounded by green curtains. There was an electroencephalogram. Nameless doctors measured their nameless patient; metrics were unclear, but the fallback conclusion was that I had had a seizure. That was the entry point for a long series of tests as they tried to figure out what was wrong with me. I wondered if perhaps I had actually had a seizure, but I was too afraid and ashamed to say anything. It felt the same as when I was a child. I was voiceless, on this occasion partially by choice but mostly by being subsumed into the emergency room system with its emphasis on rapid diagnosis and treatment.

I waited. And I took this time to consider what had happened. I was not thinking about why I had chosen to do what I did. It was done. I'd had no plan after hitting the floor. The doctors were manufacturing the plan. Simply because of the way I looked, they would never conceive of the possibility that I was dissembling. I was ground down physically and emotionally and spiritually and they had no way to measure that.

I was released with a prescription for Dilantin, which I flushed down the toilet.

For the next year and a half, I wore the emotional garb of someone who was disabled and a victim. I was treated with care. But it was not the answer. It was horrible. I did not even get much rest, even though I was supposed to. I would wake up when my roommate comrades left for work and lie there, spasming with guilt, my conscience clawing at me. I had never allowed myself to see myself as ill. So now, had I manufactured illness or revealed some underlying illness? Why had I not been able to claim illness previously? But despite my guilt, in a manipulative and secretive way I believed I had also bought myself some time to rest and heal.

Still, I became increasingly despondent and feared I was losing my intelligence and memory. I went to a psychologist, who tested me and said I was in the ninety-ninth percentile for memory and intelligence. But, he added, even though I had not come to him for that purpose, he felt obligated to tell me that in his professional opinion I was suffering from severe chronic depression. I felt his diagnosis was an effort to undermine my willpower and self-discipline and so ignored it. The party would not have allowed it anyway. It was a *petit-bourgeois* judgment. The real question was: Should I choose to stand on the side of the proletariat or the bourgeoisie? To stand on the side of the proletariat was to decide to always be self-critical based on the criterion of what would benefit the working class, and of course, what benefited the party was what benefited the working class. Ideology trumps a psychological diagnosis every time.

After about eighteen months, Claudia, the leader at the party's publishing house, started getting on my case. She felt I was not being a true cadre, not being resolute. I don't remember the exact nature of her criticisms. I just remember having the feeling that she saw through me. Which she did.

At a branch meeting, I endured a lengthy criticism session. My comrades also felt something was wrong, that I was off in some way, but they could not put their finger on it. It was similar to the way in which criticisms would be raised about sexism, when it was okay to simply say the overt or covert sexism being practised was driving you crazy. Often, that sort of intuition-based approach turned out to have some foundation. On the other hand, you could find sexism and racism anytime, anywhere, and as time went by this purely subjective approach was subject to increasing abuse as leadership became more corrupt.

There was no conclusion reached in my criticism session, nothing punitive: "We will continue this another time, comrade." We went on a break. The branch officers congregated in a downstairs bedroom to confer on how the meeting was going (the term for this process was *collectivizing*). I fidgeted upstairs, not talking with my comrades. Eventually, my discomfort, my conscience and my Catholic brain pushed me to tell the truth. I knocked on the bedroom door. Diane, the branch executive officer, answered.

She looked at me. "Yes?"

I said, "I faked my collapse and have been lying to the party." The officers looked at me, stunned. Diane asked me to repeat what I had just said. I did. She told me to go to my room and stay there. I did, waiting hours until the end of the meeting.

"Comrade Delaney (we used aliases as a security practice), you have lied to the party. We expect total honesty and you have betrayed our trust. You are on punitive suspension until further notice. You will not communicate with any of your comrades and they will not communicate with you. You should spend time thinking about your crimes."

Shunned and isolated, I stayed at home, cleaning the house and studying *The Training of the Cadre*. I was in suspended animation. It wasn't long before leadership realized that my method of punishment was just what I had apparently been trying to achieve through my dissembling. So I was the first person in the history of the party to be put on "working suspension." I had to report to my assignment at the same time as everyone else and put in a whole day of work but never talk with anyone, except to acknowledge that I understood the assignments I was given.

The party leadership did not know what to do with me. I had told the truth. That was just as amazing as the fact that I had lied for almost two years. Lying to the party was always considered the gravest crime. Ostensibly, no one had ever lied as egregiously as I had. And no one had ever told the truth the way I had.

The party gathered the people considered most likely to affect me: Barbara, a former lover. My friend David. My physician Tom. Yvonne and Richard from leadership. They all confronted me at a meeting. David mocked me for pretending to be like St. Francis. Tom calculated the wasted thousands of dollars' worth of health care I had received. It was a surreal, quasi-Zen exercise.

Yvonne said, "Don't be so melodramatic, Delaney!"

As soon as she said that, I noted the speed at which it had come out of her and the fact that I had not yet been that melodramatic. (Recall, this was by the standards of a communist organization, where *melodramatic* was used to describe any expression of human feelings). I knew that she and Richard had been briefed on how to deal with me. I recognized the implementation of guidance from above.

What could I say? Shame had been part of my daily life since childhood. I was on some weird spiritual journey, one that only an ex-Catholic could take. I now can see my collapse as giving myself over to fate, as putting myself in the hands of God.

Three years after my "confession," I was living with roommates in the Park Slope neighbourhood of Brooklyn and was part of the New York branch. The party had entered its dying days, but we in New York were not yet cognizant of what was happening in San Francisco headquarters. We laboured on. One day, as I returned to our apartment, I reached for the door and just as I grasped the filigreed doorknob, the image of my mother lying on the kitchen floor in front of the stove hit me, and I saw that I had been behaving just as my mother had.

Mom had us seven children and held a full-time job outside the house from the time that Teresa, the youngest, entered school. She woke at 6:00 a.m., turned on the percolator and began a workday that lasted until 9:30 p.m. Not too different from my life as a communist. Mom never quit.

She worked until she dropped. Which she did periodically. We'd be getting ready for supper, several of us kids setting the table, helping out. Mom would be at the stove. Soundlessly, she would slip to the floor, straight down into a heap. We knew what to do. Kathy went to get Dad. Mike turned off the stove. I got the small saucepan from the lower cabinet. Kevin got the hypodermic needle. We started boiling the needle. Dad came and propped Mom up, got her to a sitting position on the floor and injected her with B12. After half an hour or so, everything was normal.

I stayed in the party, and my life there was similar to my mother's. Early rising, a highly productive and focused day, and when the work was done and I was ready to drop, alcohol turned off the day and pushed doubts and fears into a fitful dream world.

Standing at the Back Door of Happiness, Part 3

The Door Swings Open

Before being sent to the Milwaukee branch in early 1985, I was interviewed by Rosa, the party's second in command. I told her I thought I was alcoholic. She poo-pooed the idea. I was the first person to out the beast of alcoholism in the party. But I was not important enough to be listened to, let alone acknowledged.

A few months later, another party member injured himself severely while drunk. Then alcoholism began to be taken more seriously. The organization began crumbling during 1985 as truths were slowly faced.

I had been in the New York branch for six months. We could see the internal signs of change but had no idea what they meant. Weird things were happening. At one branch meeting the function of the branch leader was deconstructed and found to be meaningless. Not long after, everyone was called back to San Francisco for a meeting of the whole party, which at that point had about 125 cadres.

Rosa was the chair. She informed us that Marlene Dixon was in Bulgaria. She told the story of Dixon's alcoholism and the enabling done by those around her. Over the course of a few hours, the life I had led for the last ten years was killed and dissected. We voted, first, to expel Marlene Dixon from the party. We did that to make ourselves believe that we were powerful. Second, we voted to dissolve the party. We walked out, free at last.

I did not know what my future held. I was indeed free but a day previously I had been a true believer. I knew I had to return to San Francisco, where my friends were. I had to reconnect and rebuild my relationship with my daughter. I stayed in New York for a couple more weeks. I went to a Knicks game at Madison Square Garden. I ate lots of pizza slices. I went to the Cloisters. I met my friend Bill at the Museum of Modern Art. And then I left for a new life in San Francisco.

Two days after my arrival, I was walking through the UN Plaza when I saw Gary Titus. Tall, handsome, warm-hearted, wise Gary. I gave a little leap of joy and ran to him. His handsome face began working as he walked toward me and then that face collapsed into something almost unrecognizable. Some spirit shone through, hideous and lovely and indescribable, and he grabbed onto me as if I were a life raft and he would never let go. His six-foot-three-inch body spasmed and I did not know what was going on and he roared out a low sob and then another and then he said, "Jon has AIDS and I need you to help."

I was overwhelmed with grief. The entire AIDS epidemic washed through me, my heart crying out for all the dying men, for all the lives being taken, for Jon's impending death.

In that instant, my life began to change, to take a turn

toward happiness. I stepped out of a world of criticism and harsh judgment into a world of love and death.

"Yes," I told Gary, "I will help." This was not a difficult choice. I wanted to help. But what could I do in the face of AIDS? What could anyone do?

Out of the party, I weighed 115 pounds and smoked two packs of Kents (they *were* low tar, you know) and up to a pint of Royal Gate Lemon-Flavored Vodka every day. I wasn't alcoholic because I only drank at night. Mostly. Except at social events. Or when I had a cold or the flu, which was an excuse for a few days of bingeing while I was in bed recovering. I was like my mom, who worked twelve hours a day and didn't drink until the news came on at night, or like my brother Kevin who didn't drink until he got off his shift as a cook at midnight. I subsisted on coffee, pastries and burritos.

I knew these were physical manifestations of a spiritual problem. I knew part of my soul was missing, but what good did it do to know that? I did not know what part had shrivelled or what to do about it.

And yet, always people loved me. And love rescued me.

Jon Herzstam had been born and raised a Christian Scientist, and that background, long discarded, reared up when he was diagnosed with AIDS. In a bizarre iteration of Christian Science, Jon believed he had something besides AIDS, yet when that was proved untrue, he still believed it. It was horrible to see hope on faces, and you felt a lump in your stomach as you listened and then offered whatever love you had in the form of awkward, hideously formed sentences. But when you hugged you could give love; your body and your heart could do what your brain could not.

Until finally, now, Jon had asked for hospice. His friends,

whose care he had spurned because it would have meant he was dying of AIDS, were at the ready. I told Gary I would organize the volunteers who would help Jon.

Our first meeting, at Jon and Gary's house on Day Street, was attended by a dozen willing friends. This was my first taste of how the gay and lesbian communities were responding with love and service to the AIDS epidemic. Jon's sister Suzanne arrived at the meeting uninvited and extremely drunk. She completely disrupted the gathering, but people there were understanding of her grief. I was stunned by the acceptance and love, so diametrically opposite of the Democratic Workers Party ethos.

After the meeting, Kitsy, the hospice social worker, requested a separate meeting with Jon and me. Jon lay on the couch and Kitsy sat next to him. I was across the room.

"Jon, I want you to tell me about your family. You have two sisters?"

Jon looked puzzled; his brow wrinkled. He looked as though he was ready to say something that was not quite ready to emerge. Kitsy waited and then said, "One sister is Suzanne." Jon nodded but still wrestled with his response.

I interjected. "Jon, Heather lives in Boulder." He looked irritated.

Kitsy gestured for my silence and repeated, "One sister is Suzanne." Jon's face worked; he was trying.

Again I tried to step in. "Kitsy, he has another sister in Colorado ..." Kitsy turned and pushed both of her palms abruptly toward me. I finally caught on that my explanation was neither desired nor needed.

She turned again to face Jon and after a long moment she said, "Are you trying to say that one sister is Suzanne when she's sober, and another is Suzanne when she's drunk?" Jon lit up and nodded.

Afterward I asked Kitsy, "How did you know that?" and she said, "Well, you have to listen really well."

And so, my tendency to judge and make corrections began to recede from my life.

I had arrived in this loving community in my own broken state, a true believer. No, not a true believer, a true doer posing as a true believer. An emotional zombie. I knew, I just knew that my problem was spiritual in nature, but I did not know what to do about it.

I went from a life where I heard constant criticism, where I was expected to be self-critical, where our organization's goal was to change the world for the better, where I worked incessantly, to a world where in the face of AIDS people pulled together and helped each other and loved each other, where people fought for the right to life and to health care while simultaneously understanding that some people wanted to choose to die. Where hospice care grew, and new families grew as former families shrivelled and died, where life was a death watch charged with love. I was loved for who I was and what I could bring. Which was love. Love long repressed. Love come alive. I had stumbled through the back door of happiness.

I Don't Understand Why I Didn't Understand

I don't understand why I didn't understand what was happening. I understand now. I think. Or you might say I understand somewhat better. But back then? Not so.

David should have been dead. I thought it was a death watch down in LA. That was why I was there. He had no muscle mass left. His insides ... he couldn't eat anything but Jell-O. For a couple of months or more. He had a huge diaper but there was nothing left to shit. It was just there to catch blood. His mouth was filled with thrush, all white and dry. When he talked, every word meant something. You really listened.

I loved David Kleinberg. We were opposites in many ways. Me: small, with a facial difference. Lots of emotional armour. Good Catholic boy. My nickname: Tidy Boy.

David: tall, heavy, a bear, handsome. Gay. Adventurous. He loved to cook. Once he sprinkled oregano in the crème brûlée. He roamed San Francisco in the 1970s, roamed the city hard. He loved going to the Ritch Street baths where he spent evenings strapped into a harness, face down, naked, with his legs apart, exposed to the open door of a cubicle where men could wander in and fuck him in the ass.

I was drawn to his vibrant charm, his giggle, his capacity for intimacy. He would come up behind me, reach around and play with my nipples. I trusted him. I liked it. That was good practice for emotional openness and a sense of adventure.

Now he was dying in West Hollywood. He had a lover, Bob, a TV producer of shows like *Nine to Five* and *Mr. Belvedere*. After they got serious, David began nesting and his tastes changed from opera to *The Golden Girls*. He had an autographed photo of Estelle Getty on his dresser. He became a Dodger fan because Bob loved baseball. Now David had AIDS. As he began to slip, I began flying down to LA on weekends whenever I could to help out.

I wanted to help, but I was so afraid. I did not even know how afraid I was. I had recently quit drinking, and the decades-long practice of dissolving my emotions in alcohol was no longer available.

I was afraid of what I saw when I stood in the doorway of David's Westwood apartment and looked at him on the daybed. No more burly. No more flesh. Bone. One leg drawn up, the femur almost devoid of flesh, like something from a Francis Bacon portrait, as if he had just pulled his leg away from piranhas. The whole image of him that had existed in my mind gone—as though it had been Photoshopped away. His diaper, huge, the biggest I had ever seen, like something you would see in a cartoon. All bone and diaper until he opened his eyes and they were unchanged, still warm and brown and deep.

I was afraid of the smell. The diaper, yes, for sure. Worse, the metallic reek of medication on his breath. Worst of all, the aroma of necrotic tissue, of wasted flesh, of David's death a 90 percent done deal, his GI tract dying out his asshole, death breath rising from his body, death soaked into everything—the walls, the carpet, the drapes, imbuing all the fabrics, clinging to the dishes. Every Sunday night I carried that smell with me to the airport, onto the plane, back to San Francisco.

Afraid of the sounds. Every breath a choice, any one could be his last choice, dry, raspy, thrushy sounds or wet gurgles, every breath challenged and precious.

My hands on David felt no flesh; they went from skin to bone. Some parts of him were cold and damp, some hot and damp, some hot and dry; some felt festering beneath the skin, some chilling toward death.

What I tasted when I kissed his forehead was like nothing I ever tasted before.

And yet. The fear was overwhelmed by amazement that he was still alive. Every day for months, he could be dead that night. But he was not.

And how was it that he was so beautiful? Everything he had left was in his eyes. And heart.

In my fear, I wanted to know the rules. I wanted to help.

"Hi, David. What do you need? Just tell me. Anything. What should I do? I know! Jell-O. I'll make Jell-O. We'll have Jell-O. Lemon-lime or black cherry. Which?"

"Just be here."

"There's Cool Whip!"

"Just be here."

Shut the fuck up, I thought desperately. *Eat the fucking Jell-O, pass the time away until you die. You are supposed to die. Somebody said so. That's the rule. That's the procedure. That's the protocol.*

All he had was presence. All he had was love. All he had was touch. All he wanted was touch. All he wanted was love. All he wanted was presence.

Ignore the body, see the soul. No choice, I had no choice. I could not find any other rules that applied.

The moment of change: when I opened the Jell-O, the black cherry Jell-O, and it smelled worse than death and it made me sick. I preferred the smell of death. More real. I didn't understand. What was going on?

At first I thought he was not in touch with his needs or was too shy to say what he really wanted. Or, worst of all, perhaps he had the AIDS dementia we had heard about. It took me weeks to understand that he knew exactly what he needed. He wanted my full presence. I learned to shut up. Then we could sit for hours, saying nothing at all. We listened to music that he loved—the Mass in B Minor. Marvin Gaye. And opera, of course. (Gay, dying of AIDS? Let's put "Un bel dì, vedremo" on repeat.)

By then, David wasn't talking much anyway. One thing he did say, every day and for no apparent reason was "Good for you. Good for you."

It was a Sunday evening. We were on the couch together. My suitcase was packed and near the door. I was ready to leave for San Francisco and work the next morning. David's head was on my lap. I had been stroking his forehead and my hand rested there. His eyes were closed. Occasionally pain broke through the drugs and made him twitch and gasp. David was silent; I thought he was asleep. Then I felt his body slowly gathering energy. He smacked his lips, trying to bring moisture to his mouth. He opened his eyes and stared at the far wall for a very long moment. He turned his face up toward me.

"Could you stay for the rest of the week?"

I drew my hand away and started to explain why that could not possibly happen. I'd be fired.

I stopped. I was flooded with the knowledge that I did want to simply be there. That was a moment of grace for me. I didn't make a choice. It was given to me—a moment of absolute clarity when love took priority. David had pulled me into that moment. "Yes," I said softly.

David took my hand back, kissed the palm, held it to his heart and said, "Good for you."

He closed his eyes and turned away, breathing deeply. As he dozed off again, I felt his heart slowing in my hand.

That was the last week of David's life. The moment of grace he gave me changed my life. I understood. He wanted music, he wanted touch, most of all he lived for love. It wasn't a death watch. It was a love watch.

I loved the manner in which he died. He glowed into death. He rotted and glowed. His body rotted, his soul glowed. His soul grew and filled the room. He was getting his soul ready. We bathed in his soul.

I wasn't fired. My co-workers at the City and County of San Francisco told me to take whatever time I needed. So I could stand there at the graveside and watch the jacaranda blossoms drift into his grave and be covered with dirt.

It Was Sin
that Saved My Soul:
The Overlap of Love
and Death

I t was sin that brought me fully into the human race. It was
sin that saved my soul.

In the late 1980s, Marlena and I were co-founders of
the massage program at Pacific Presbyterian Hospital in San
Francisco. It was the first hospital-based massage therapy program in the United States.

Hospital massage is the gentlest possible. Tenderness and
care are necessary when your hands venture amid tubes and
needles and bandages and pain and strange happenings and,
often, the nearness of death.

After our initial period of training, of absorbing protocols
and techniques, we still had more to learn. The first time I
volunteered on the Planetree unit, the charge nurse sent me
in to offer Mr. Jenkins a massage. "He's been quite agitated,"
she said. I did not know what that meant. I walked into 15B,
a standard single room. There was Mr. Jenkins—elderly,
very thin, in his hospital gown, sitting in a hospital-issue

orange Naugahyde armchair with his IV pole next to him. He seemed rather calm for someone who was "quite agitated."

"Hi, I'm David, I'm a volunteer. Would you like a massage?"

"Yes." He lifted up his gown and spread his legs apart, revealing a bright-red rash on the inside of each thigh right up to his genitals. He handed me the jar of Eucerin that had been sitting on the windowsill. Of course, I was stunned. My first thought was *Wow, if Saint Francis can kiss a leper, I can do this.* That was what came into my head, and I immediately calmed down. I took a gloop of the Eucerin and massaged that flaming rash on the inside of Mr. Jenkins's thighs. His rash, rough and warm to the touch, was him, and my hands were me. What was real was the connection between us, not sexual but very intimate. Any judgment, any concern about agitation, had faded. This was an act of love—a good beginning for what became eight years of being a massage therapist. I learned that when you are a hospital patient, modesty is pretty much a disposable virtue.

The charge nurse looked at me as I emerged from 15B. I nodded to her. She handed me Mr. Jenkins's chart, wherein I wrote, "Patient appreciated massage."

Walking into a hospital room was entering into the patient's personal and total world. Beds, tubes, bedding, IV poles and bags, all were similar from room to room. The individual in the bed defined that world, and it was important to enter into it on their terms as much as possible. When I watched physicians stepping into that world for the first time, I saw how their eyes assessed and absorbed it all—or at least the medical aspects. We knew the medical assessment of each person we served, but the rest was up to us. Sometimes it was difficult to take in what we first saw.

The whites of Jim Steinemann's eyes were a lurid yellow; his entire body was bloated and yellow. He had received a stem-cell transplant. Sometimes the body rejects such a transplant; in his case, the transplant was in the process of rejecting his body. Jim was in Pacific Presbyterian Hospital simply waiting to die. His pain was the kind that only death would ease. Whenever, wherever he was touched he'd writhe and scream in pain. We were brought to him in hopes we could bring some element of comfort to his final days. I was chosen to try. Jim lay on his back breathing shallowly to avoid the pain that deeper breathing brought. I approached that swollen yellow flesh slowly, with as much intention and openness as I could muster. I did not know what I was doing; I had to strip away all thoughts, to get out of my brain. I held my hands an inch above his leg, waiting for that sacred moment of trust and openness and connection between two humans. He did not scream. I was able to touch him, to stay in that precious zone of tenderness and love and to offer some temporary relief, to get through what we called the *pain gate*.

We were in San Francisco in the time of the AIDS epidemic; in the hospital, people were dying of AIDS, ALS, cancer, of usual and unusual conditions. This was the world that Marlena and I were drawn to, that we thrived in, the milieu where our relationship was born, nurtured and formed. When death is standing near, priorities become clear and little time is wasted in small talk. Intimacy, especially when expressed in tender touch, was the valued currency of love.

Patients often told us that it was not medical treatment but massage that had healed them. I accepted such comments as simply being expressions of courtesy and gratitude. Now I have a different understanding. With our hands we brought love that was healing.

Over time, this deeply physical experience formed the core of my spirituality. It was highly tactile, relational, intimate, innately transparent, often with people who knew they were on the verge of dying. This environment nourished me, let me become my best and deepest self. For me, spirituality is of the flesh, entirely incarnational, and that is what grew in me.

This was rooted in my Roman Catholic childhood and four years of studying to be a priest. The nuns at Our Lady of Grace School told us that we were children of God, that we were souls and that our souls lived, ensconced inside us. At the core of Catholic theology is belief in the Incarnation, that God became flesh in the form of Jesus Christ. Humanity became sacralized through that Incarnation. One strain of Catholicism, born under the tutelage of Paul and his devotees, turned toward self-flagellation, sexual repression and bitter misogyny. A healthier and more loving Catholic meme lives in the Corporal Works of Mercy, wherein love is embodied, concretely real. Jesus exemplified the spirituality of touch (and storytelling). Thus, my epiphanous moment of remembering that Saint Francis of Assisi kissed a leper was immediately and highly motivational and unquestioned for me. Even with no sense of God as being an actual entity, I experienced the sacred in my work.

In the year prior to beginning the hospital massage, I had undergone a deep physical, emotional and intellectual crisis by having put my soul on loan for twelve years as a dedicated Marxist-Leninist-Maoist cadre. I had wanted to help change the world and end the cruelty of the rich. At the end of that time of stress, striving and frustration, I was underweight, drank in excess, smoked two packs of cigarettes a day and lots of dope and, needless to say, ate unhealthy food.

I recognized that I was having a spiritual crisis and knew I had to first reclaim and then rebuild my soul. I retried Catholicism, then Buddhism and Judaism. None offered a new start. On my own (or so I thought), I began to see that what nurtured my soul daily was threefold: nature, loving relationships and creativity. I prided myself on discovering and claiming my own spirituality. Hurray for me! Then I saw that this was what the nuns had tried to teach me about the Trinity, that there were three persons in one God. My eight-year-old brain could only imagine a Hydra-headed divinity. But now I had three ways of experiencing the divine, the sacred in my life: in nature (God the father, the creator), in relationships (Jesus, the son of God, was relational and loving) and in creativity (the inspiration of the Holy Spirit). It was there at Pacific Presbyterian Hospital that I got all three on a regular basis.

It was there that I met Marlena.

We began our relationship in this community built around service and caring as manifested in touch. And we slowly, slowly fell in love. We lured, seduced and danced around each other for half a year of wonderful foreplay (though we did not recognize it as such).

For the first time, in this new environment, my facial difference, up until then an unacknowledged presence in my life, was called forward. I had never talked about my face. It was a secret. Marlena, out of respect for my way of dealing with my life (and also some of her own shyness) had never asked me about it. I certainly didn't want anybody touching me there. Why would they want to? But when we practised, she had me on the massage table and I was the patient being healed. She touched my face, went courageously and lovingly into that forbidden territory.

My face is very sensitive. Marlena said, "It's like you have a breast I can fondle." She touched nerves, ligaments, everything as I lay emotionally naked on the table. Marlena was teaching me, integrating me with myself. What was happening was all new to me. My brain did not understand but my cells did.

After a beloved friend died, Marlena offered a massage to help me deal with my grief. It lasted two hours; I was completely in my body, although strangely, my body seemed to have expanded to fill half the room. When she was done, I said I wanted to give her a massage. After about fifteen minutes, I bent and kissed her. That is the number one "you'd better not" in the world of bodywork. Marlena said, "Don't. I'm married." That seemed so very irrelevant to me. I drew back, but the bridge had been crossed. My grief had been dealt with; it had become desire.

The intensity of grief, the intensity of love. How could I resist my own vulnerability? Marlena had slowly seduced me, and I had finally responded. I was at one with myself, sure of myself. My earlier doubts about adultery and infidelity had shallow roots.

Marlena had said, "Don't," but a few days later she called to invite me to dinner at a Thai restaurant on Mission near 30th. It was crowded, and we sat at the bar. I don't remember what we talked about, but I do recall being aware of her breathing and mine being in magical synchrony. After dinner we walked up the Bernal Hill stairs. At the crest we turned and walked to a point where we watched the fog rolling in over Twin Peaks while the sun shone above the fog on the East Bay. All the windows in Oakland glimmered in that summer sun and shined on us. We held each other for a long moment, aligning our desires. I bent and kissed her, that long-awaited kiss, more than a kiss, a kiss without question, filled with that desire.

Yes, Marlena was married when our relationship began. When we first met, I was hesitant, doubtful, self-judging. But that was all in my brain, and for me, thoughts are basically the fecal matter of my brain. Within a short time magnetism trumped moralism, we were lovers and I was qualm-free. No second thoughts. I knew we were having an affair (duh!) but I had no sense of doing anything wrong. *Affair* was a meaningless word. And if this was a sin then I loved sin. I revelled in the lack of self-judgment. I thought, *Oh my God, I have finally joined the human race. And sin has saved my soul.*

The Angel of Frozen Time

I was apprehensive the first time I stepped through the front door of Leo and Lillian's house in Skokie, Illinois. This would be my first meeting with my mother- and father-in-law to be. Marlena's ex, Larry, had been a successful financial analyst. And he was Jewish. As a facially disfigured comedian, I was not as financially successful. I had an Irish Catholic background. And a unique face, with swollen purple veins colouring its left half.

The first thing I noticed in their house was that the Angel of Frozen Time had been a visitor in the early 1970s. Gliding through each room, the Angel had swept her arm (in a counterclockwise motion, of course) and frozen in time all objects therein.

In the living room, a heavy jade ashtray on the coffee table was never to be moved, never to be used. Little crystal animals on the credenza were locked in place. Above the sofa, a colourful, vaguely cubist painting of a jazz combo, the saxophone player leaning forward into his instrument, had apparently been a symbol of Skokie hip for decades.

In the bathroom, brown towels, never actually touched, were folded just so. Pink and gold wall tiles gleamed clean. In the medicine cabinet, the huge jar of Vaseline had darkened slightly with each decade. On the bottom, a barely legible price tag: "Rexall Drugs. 55¢." By now it was practically a family heirloom.

In the kitchen, the appliances were the same colour as the Vaseline. A sunburst wall clock had kept perfect time for half a century.

And so, too, the living patterns of Leo and Lil had acquired a certain constancy. When I married Marlena, I stepped into that world and found a new family.

As the eldest of seven children, my background was different. I love my family dearly, but we were not as woven together in the same ways as Marlena's. When she and I first met, I noticed she called her parents every couple of weeks, no matter what was going on in her life. If she didn't call Leo and Lil on a regular basis, they began to worry.

"Marlena, where have you been? Why haven't you called? We were so worried. We saw that fire on TV."

"Mom, I live in San Francisco. That was in Los Angeles." ‘

I mentioned to Marlena that it was probably time for me to give my father a call. She asked, "Has it been a while?"

I said, "Oh, maybe five or six years." She laughed, thinking I was joking. I had been estranged from my father for years; there never seemed to be a reason to talk.

The easiest adjustment in my new family was to food. My first visit was the excuse for Leo to go to Kaufman's Deli and get bagels and lox and cream cheese. And smoked whitefish and pickled tomatoes. And smoked chubs, which apparently had looked very fresh and plump in the display case. And just a little corned beef.

When Leo delivered the deli shipment, Lil's kitchen table was the loading dock. She removed the white-paper-wrapped goodies from the bag and arranged them on the table. She felt each one and sniffed it before opening. Leo had immediately busied himself at the other end of the house.

"Leo!" she called out. "Leo, corned beef! Pastrami! You know you are not supposed to have this."

Leo stuck his head around the corner: "Lil, it's for David. You can't get pastrami like that in San Francisco."

And there were prune Danishes. And a huge chunk of halvah. Oh yes, the pickles. All things usually forbidden to Leo. As his official excuse, I was a very welcome guest. The deli spread became a tradition that he and I both delighted in.

At our first dinner together, Leo and Marlena and I sat at the dining room table as Lil served. My mother, with her full-time job in addition to all her children, had not had much time to cook, and all us kids took turns preparing simple suppers. One of our great treats was canned potatoes. Irish potatoes, we called them. In Skokie, it was homemade latkes. "With real sour cream … for David."

Initially, I was shocked at the seemingly endless bickering at the dinner table. At my childhood dinner table, the dance had been an Irish reel of verbal sallies, often edged, but softened with humour and rushes of laughter. Here, the conversation consisted of a more straightforward pattern of accusation and defense; sometimes the dining room seemed like a courtroom.

As Lil brought a new package of napkins to the dinner table, she exclaimed, "Leo, you didn't use the coupons for the paper towels!" She held out the price sticker and receipt as evidence.

Leo was ready and waiting. He had the coupons at hand in his pocket and pulled them out. "Lil, here, take a look at them. They are expired. You gave me expired coupons." He presented them to me as defense exhibit A (a futile gesture, as I did not have my reading glasses). Leo, however, apparently decided that the fact of my accepting the coupons constituted proof of some sort.

He turned to Marlena and upped the ante. "See what your mother asks me to do?"

Lil was a little flustered by the vigorous counterattack, but if she was confident about anything in the world, it was her knowledge of coupons. She was a couponologist. In a moment she reassessed the evidence and deftly presented the prosecution's theory. "Where did you get those? Where did they come from? Leo, you didn't take these from the table. You are supposed to take them from the table. Why on earth—"

"They were in my pocket. Right where they—"

"In your pocket? Oh, for God's sake, Leo. I can't believe it." She turned to Marlena. "He's had them in his pocket for two weeks!" She turned back to Leo. "Why don't you look at the coupons? You have to take them from the pile on the table. You know you have to take them from the table." She looked at me and shook her head sadly.

Leo offered the last gurgle of the drowning defendant. "They were expired."

Then came a few moments of domestic joy as Leo and Lil explained the wonderful world of Happy Foods coupons to us. They exclaimed about $1.29 apple pies and ground beef for sixty-nine cents a pound. Still, the bickering had an inevitable quality, ebbing and swelling like the waves on Lake Michigan.

"Sixty-nine cents! And it is good ground beef too."

"Lil, you don't know if it's good. It's still in the freezer."

"I have been buying ground beef for fifty years. I know good ground beef."

Then there was a brief moment of blissful agreement on how wonderful it was to live around the corner from Happy Foods. "Especially in the wintertime."

This observation provided a natural segue; there are so many entry points to bickering.

"Leo, you have to talk to Angelo about shovelling the driveway. I don't want you out there this winter."

"I will, I will. Lil, this is August."

Now, of course, Marlena and I bicker all the time. We both have an inner Leo and an inner Lil, but I often have Lil's role. "Honey, why don't you eat the rest of that soup? Just eat it or we'll have to throw it out. Please don't make me waste it."

I believe that bickering is one of the keys to a successful marriage. All those resentments and judgments—if you get them out immediately, they won't build up.

"Marlena, are you going to just leave this pile of papers and crap on the table?"

I try to protect Marlena from imagined dangers. "Drive carefully. Promise me. Did you hear me?"

The Angel of Frozen Time also kept Marlena as a fifteen-year-old—at least in the eyes of Leo and Lillian. They still saw her wearing hip huggers and trying to straighten her curly hair with empty frozen-orange-juice cans. The world had changed. Their love for Marlena had not changed, but it was by no means an uncritical love. One of our many visits illustrated this well.

Marlena was forty-eight years old—chronologically. But not in the home that time forgot. On this visit, she decided she wanted to visit her high school boyfriend and his family one evening, a social event that did not interest me at all. I begged off, stayed home and went to bed early. At 11:00 p.m. I was awakened by persistent rapping at my bedroom door. It was Leo.

"David, sorry to wake you up. She's not home yet! We have to do something!"

"Leo, there's not a problem. I'm sure she'll be home soon."

I thought I had offered Leo some reassurance. I rolled over and went back to sleep. Just before midnight, I was awakened again. This time there was no knocking. Leo burst into the room. "We have to call the hospitals."

I persuaded them not to call the hospitals or the police. I went back to bed but could not sleep. I could hear them pacing up and down the hallway, chanting fear and anger like a mantra. "Lil, you will have to deliver the reprimand."

At 12:30 I heard the front door opening. Leo and Lil scurried into their bedroom and shut the door. In three beats they were out again, in full recriminative mode, down the hall to the living room where they confronted their forty-eight-year-old teenager. "You haven't changed a bit! Just like in high school! Why didn't you call? The police have been searching for you." (Not true.)

Marlena's defenses, her tone of voice, seemed strangely juvenile to me. "I didn't say when I would be home. You didn't set a curfew. You have to trust me." She was being sucked into the vortex of eternal adolescence.

What I had seen as overparenting suddenly took on a different cast when my daughter, Amy, arrived back from Israel in the summer of 2001. She landed at O'Hare after twenty-four hours of travelling and several missed connections. Her flight was ten hours late and the friends who were to meet her had to leave. On short notice, Leo was there at O'Hare to get her. By the time they got back to Skokie, Lil had hot lentil soup and bread on the table. The bed was made up—the same one Marlena used to sleep in. The brown towels were out for a hot bath. Amy, at age thirty-eight, was taken care of just as if she were fifteen years old.

Not only did Amy now have new grandparents, I recognized that I had been given a new set of parents. God bless you, Leo and Lil. Mom and Dad.

Genius, Player, Elder

For five years I taught storytelling at The Foundry, a public high school for at-risk students in San Jose, California. The lead teacher was John Malloy, who had spent years as an inmate at San Quentin. He and his colleagues devoted their lives to the kids. It was a tough-love, follow-the-rules-or-you-are-out program.

The Foundry, although part of the San Jose public school system, followed Lakota spirituality. We held long-distance runs, and students often camped out in the Sierra Nevada. There was a Lakota emphasis on the importance of the environment in forming and building character. Circle gatherings started and ended each day.

I had been used to adult storytellers reviewing their lives and now had to get used to adolescents. Their stories were about pregnancy, fear of pregnancy, pride at becoming pregnant, appearances in juvenile court, stays at juvenile hall, parole-officer meetings and more. Their stories were told in all sorts of styles: weeping, scornful, despairing, cocky, fearful, proud. These kids lived the stories as they told them, as they strove to find themselves. Their life-review stories were days old. All their stories had love in them in some way: the search for love, the rejection of love, the love of family.

My favourite Foundry day began as I listened to Michael Krasny's *Forum* on KQED-FM on the drive down from San Francisco. My friend Annie Lamott was a guest and they were discussing whether she was a genius. Annie demurred and remarked, "David Roche is a genius." Krasny agreed with her. What a wonderful compliment! I liked it even better when I arrived at The Foundry and one of the new students was taken aback by my facial difference. He was not rude, just surprised, the way people often are upon first encountering me face to face. They need a couple of minutes to adjust and sometimes to stare. Then I heard some of the guys tell him that I was a *playah*. What? Where did they get that notion? But I wasn't complaining. Wow—called out as a genius and a playah on the same day!

I was a little anxious as it was the first day of winter/spring semester, one of those crystal-bright Beach Boys days when a rainstorm had cleared the smog out of the air. A number of new students were in an unfamiliar environment, and that always brought some tension into the school.

I had arrived a little early, and students were still in home-rooms. I stopped by the office to greet friends. Johanna was volunteering on the phones, a time-consuming task on opening day. Barbara asked whether I'd read the copy of *Pay It Forward* she had sent me. We chatted for a few moments about Kevin Spacey and how the film did not convey the power of the book. Louise stood at the counter dealing with the flow of parents, social workers, probation officers and late students. When there was an opening in the stream of need, I expressed my admiration for the office redecorating. She laughed when I told her I missed the BEATINGS WILL CONTINUE UNTIL MORALE IMPROVES sign.

Kids began wandering into the office area. Returnees from last semester greeted me. Trish had a ring in her lower lip with a distinctive, beautiful blue stone in it. I complimented her taste, and her friend proudly revealed that she was the one who had given it to Trish. I loved that students were happy to see me. I also loved that they wore nametags.

When homeroom was over, we gathered in the main room, standing in a circle of about sixty students and a dozen teachers, staff, volunteers and parents. John asked all the women present, students and adults alike, to walk to the centre of the circle to introduce themselves and make one another feel welcome. They moved in with little hesitation, young and old, hugging and chatting, a vortex of female energy. A couple of the newer girls were shy, standing on the perimeter, entranced by the welcoming atmosphere, and the circle gathered them in.

The men were asked to do the same welcoming ritual. I stepped forward into a group of some thirty-five inner-city high school boys, wondering what they thought of a grey-haired disfigured guy old enough to be their grandfather. I wanted to set an example. We shook hands, greeted each other, and did a reasonably good job of shoulder-hugging. There was a little arm punching too; it was sincere and even somewhat affectionate.

John asked the women to comment on how the men had done. They noted that we were a little reticent but gave us credit for showing good spirits.

As John continued speaking, I locked into his cadences and energy rather than his words and began to absorb my surroundings. The winter sun was low enough to fill the room with light. Almost half the students were brand new, the men outnumbering the women. It was difficult to assess class based on clothing style or general appearance. For sure there were no preppies. There was as much commonality as difference in this diverse student body. These were so-called at-risk students, most all with lives marked by the wounds that seem so common in contemporary urban adolescence: violence, substance abuse, abandonment, racism. For most of them, The Foundry was the school of last resort.

I felt my heart opening. The beginning of the semester was my special time here, and I had a role to fill.

There was a special brightness in the eyes of the students that day. Each semester, the mixture of students was different. An important startup task was building group chemistry, community and trust. John set about it. Middle aged, handsome with grey hair, square and sturdy in build, his straightforward manner matched his appearance. He and the other male teachers were strong, with open hearts—good models for what it meant to be a man.

John had been doing this for fifteen years. He was very good, getting better all the time, and it felt as though he had a solid group to work with this semester. They looked at John and at each other. Returning students projected pride and responsibility for welcoming the new ones and showing them how The Foundry worked. New students were vulnerable, looking for their place, trying to learn the culture. They knew how different this school was. Their vulnerability was one reason I was there.

John led us all outside for a stretch and a breath of fresh

air. When we returned, he and I sat on two stools and students placed themselves on the carpet in front of us. There was very little holding back; the front row filled immediately at our feet. John introduced me, and I began to talk about my experience as a disfigured person, about feeling like a monster, different from everyone else. About how I learned to find inner strength and beauty.

The Foundry was one of my spiritual homes. Here, they emphasized the very same values and practices that had strengthened me over the years and helped me to have a sense of self-worth. In the presence of these earnest young people I felt called to speak from my heart. My job was to model presence, honesty and trust. Like John, I also was getting better at what I did. I learned in my years of performing and speaking that I was not so different, that there is a commonality to the human experience. Everyone, no matter their appearance, has had to deal with some sense of either internal or external disfigurement. All have essentially the same choices as I had: stand back or step forward.

John prompted me, asking whether I would tell the story of how Marlena and I met, how Marlena heard my voice before she saw my face. She was so shocked when we were face to face that she simply walked away, but followed her heart rather than her eyes back to me. I described Marlena as being someone who saw into my soul, and John interrupted to ask the students how many of them could see the soul. Four or five raised their hands. A few minutes later, he asked how many of them felt able to take that second look at another person, just as Marlena had with me. Most raised their hands.

In front of that student body, I was looking out at a *Saturday Evening Post* cover from the 1950s. Except with a few more nose rings and tattoos. The shaved-side haircuts I saw on the boys would have seemed very familiar to Norman Rockwell, as would the diversity. And the intensity and light in their eyes. A few kids had positioned themselves off to the sides of the group, but they were gradually drawn in, and their choice of seats seemed more motivated by old habits of estrangement than current conscious rejection.

The questions started. Each one gave me pause before I answered.

Q: Have you ever wanted to kill yourself?

A: Yes, I have. Just last month. In a dark period, I found myself thinking about dying. I don't think I was suicidal, really, but I know I was thinking that if I died, then I wouldn't have to be trying so hard, and I wouldn't be afraid, and maybe I could relax.

Q: Did you like it when you got drunk?

A: Well, there is a buzz, isn't there? But there's also puking and hangovers and other stuff. When I was younger and drinking heavily, I had this joke I liked to play. I would pretend to fall down the stairs. Only one time, I really did. I tumbled down, hit the landing, spun over the balcony and fell to the floor below, smashing down onto a stack of beer glasses and an ashtray. My leg was cut open. I lay there covered with beer, blood and cigarette butts. Everyone was so drunk, they still thought it was a joke, and they stood around me and laughed. One of my friends poured whiskey on my leg to sterilize it, playing like he was a doctor. I was hurt badly and lost some of the feeling in my leg from that accident. More importantly, alcohol was covering my doubts and fears. It wasn't until I quit drinking that I found my voice and my creativity, and I got on stage and in front of groups like you.

Q: Do you believe in God?

A: Yes. Although I know not everyone calls it God. You can call it Spirit, or the universal force or higher power, qi or whatever. I say God 'cause that's what I was raised with. Here's the way I would put it: I find something sacred every day in three ways: in contact with nature, by connecting with another human being, and by using my own creativity.

Q: Do you believe God thinks you're ugly?

A: No, I don't believe that anymore. But sometimes I forget I don't believe it.

When I explained that my shadow side is on the outside where I have been forced to deal with it, John asked the students what they are hiding—what was their shadow? A dozen students responded. Marc, in the back, told us about his struggle with Attention Deficit Disorder. Alyssa stated that she was raped a few months ago. A blond girl at our feet—Danielle—said she wore long sleeves because of scars from self-mutilation. The spirit of the answers was not sensationalistic, not victim-y, but filled with trust and strength. The response of the group was silent and respectful until Julia proclaimed her three weeks of sobriety. This prompted applause and two other similar statements from others. Their life challenges were very much in the present.

I glanced at the clock. Two hours had gone by. They had been sitting on the floor with no restlessness. No one had left to use the restroom. No one had turned to comment to a friend. They had been with us—and more importantly, with one another—all the way. A sacred space had been created.

With the questions and comments done, we circled again. I stood alone in the middle, not knowing what was going to happen. John gave me a six-foot-long wooden staff and invited me to hold it upright with one hand and plant it on the floor. He directed all the new male students to come forward, grasp the pole, hold it and breathe along with me. There was a little nervous laughter and some hesitation to get as physically close as was necessary for each of them to reach to the pole. John told them to step back and try again. They did so with more ease and calmness.

Then I held the staff horizontally and the new female students came up to grasp it. John asked them to touch me in some way that felt appropriate to them. Some touched briefly and flitted away. A couple of the girls grabbed and hugged me.

Next the girls were directed to return to me one by one and tell me something privately, so no one else could hear. They whispered how handsome, how wonderful I was, how thankful they were that I was there. I glowed.

But the best had not yet happened. John called the older male students up around me. He set them in two lines, one on each side of me, then two guys at my face and two behind. Then John told these inner city, at-risk young boys to pick me up and rock me like a baby. I had a moment when I wanted to flee. I was caught strongly in that moment and found total trust inside myself. I let myself fall back. I found myself with a dozen young men holding me on my back at about waist level. I heard John: "Support his head." His voice came from a distant place. I felt a couple of hands move on my back, finding purchase. A brief wave of self-consciousness came over me as I realized that they would be looking close up at my disfigured face. Somehow, I had no fear of intimacy. The experience was so powerful, the trust so strong, that I had to submit. The rocking began. I slipped into a timeless place where I was a baby and then I was dead and being carried to my grave and then I was who I was, exactly and fully who I was, right in that time and place—an elder who had come to bring what wisdom I had to the young people. And I was being thanked and honoured by these young men with strong hands and open hearts.

It was over. I was set on my feet, strangely lighter, my whole body vibrating. John asked what I had to say, and my voice came from a distance. I turned to the guys in a circle around me, reached out and touched their chests with my fingertips. I said thank you. My entire body, my entire being had been rearranged. I was entirely different than I had been a few minutes before. I wanted to tell them this, and that they had changed my life, but somehow I was too shy and too awed by what happened to try to put it into words.

Fudge and Forgiveness

Marlena and I arrived at the Naramata retreat centre to lead a weeklong storytelling class. We brought our bags into Maple Court Residence Hall. After unpacking, I went to the common kitchen to put a leftover sandwich in the refrigerator.

I opened the freezer. Who knows why one opens a freezer for no immediately apparent reason—perhaps to check whether there will be ice cubes if needed, perhaps out of raw curiosity? Anyway, open it I did. A white paper bag sat in the door shelf. It struck my interest because it was clearly the kind of bag that candy comes in—the kind you purchase at a chocolate store. It was sort of crumpled, the kind of crumpling that was evidence of having been stashed into a purse or pocket.

Aside from two ice-cube trays, it was the only object in the freezer. I picked the bag up and hefted it. It held one squarish object, weighing maybe a quarter of a kilo. The object was firm but not hard.

Of course I was curious. Of course I opened the bag and found a piece of chocolate fudge in plastic wrap, with a label indicating it had come from a candy store in Alberta. I was in British Columbia, which meant that the fudge had made an arduous journey from another province. The plastic wrapping was slightly clouded, perhaps with some condensation underneath, the kind of condensation that could only form over a significant period of time.

Of course I did not open the package. I returned the fudge to the bag and to the freezer door.

On Monday, I didn't think much about the fudge. I was busy with the storytelling class all morning. I did have a moment or two of wondering why it had been in the freezer. Who keeps fudge in the freezer? Perhaps it stays fresher in there? But, I thought, degree of freshness is not the main attraction when it comes to fudge. Plus, in the freezer, it gets frozen. Which means you have to thaw it out before you eat it. Who wants to wait to eat fudge? It was all very puzzling.

On Tuesday, during a free moment, I realized the white bag had camouflaged the fudge because it blended in with the white interior of the freezer. Which was, I imagined, why the person who put it there had probably no doubt forgotten it. I wondered what kind of person forgets fudge, even well-camouflaged fudge. I had some sympathy for the person who certainly was now likely very possibly fudgeless in Alberta.

On Wednesday, a funny thing happened. I had been thinking about the fudge again and suddenly realized that if it belonged to someone, that person would certainly have taken it by now. A person who purchased fudge presumably liked fudge and would eat fudge. Imagine my surprise when

I happened to open the freezer door and saw that the fudge was still languishing there. Whoever had left it there clearly was not a serious fudge lover—as am I, for just one example. This person did not have strong fudge needs. It came to me that possibly I might need the fudge.

On Thursday, when the freezer door opened, the fudge was in the same place. There was no evidence that somebody cared enough about the fudge to be sure it was okay. I noticed that the edges of the fudge were rounded, as if it had been handled carelessly before being discarded in the freezer.

In the core of my being I realized that not only did I deserve the fudge, but more importantly, the fudge deserved me—a person who cared about fudge, a man who could give that fudge what it needed.

The fudge spoke to me. "Hello, big boy. Do you come here often? Listen, is it chilly in here or is it just me? Are you going to stick your hand in my bag? Oh, that's nice and warm! Do you like to eat fudge? I'll just bet you do. What do you say we go someplace where it's a little more comfortable?"

I took the fudge to my room and set it on the dresser to let it warm up. Marlena spotted it an hour or so later.

"What's this? Fudge! Where did this come from?"

"Umm, from the freezer. It had been left there some time ago."

"Honey, this is nothing but chocolate-flavoured saturated fats and sugar," said Marlena viciously.

"Or one could simply call it fudge," I responded calmly.

"Hon? You're not going to eat this, are you?"

"Perhaps not."

"I'm going to throw it out."

I said nothing for a few seconds, wondering why God had

led me to marry a fudge-hater. I sighed with dignity. "Okay."

"And I'm going to unwrap it before I throw it out. So don't bother looking for it."

I was appalled by what seemed like a lack of trust.

On Friday afternoon I was making tea in the kitchen when Corinne walked in. She was a lovely, energetic young woman who had been at the centre all week teaching world dance. She walked right to the freezer, opened the door and said, "Hey, what happened to my fudge?"

My first thought was that I should tell the honest truth and say, "I didn't eat it." But I knew that would be too similar to an untruth. I knew I had to take a higher road. "Maybe somebody cleaned out the fridge?"

"Oh, no! I was saving it for today." Corinne frowned.

I decided I had to do the right thing. "Tell you what, Corinne. Marlena and I are just about to walk to the bakery in town. Come on along and I'll buy you a brownie."

"Oh, you're so kind!"

I acknowledged her compliment with a nod and a smile.

At the bakery I bought her a piece of lemon cheesecake. She cleaned the crumbs up with her finger. "Well, that was very generous of you."

"Well, thank you, Corinne."

The way she enjoyed the cheesecake crumbs was troubling to me. All week Corinne had been working hard teaching world dance. At the end of the week she had come to get her fudge, her reward. Oh well. She got cheesecake instead. There perhaps was a way in which it was doubtless God's will.

At dinner I saw Corinne walking by. She was sweating after rehearsing for the evening's performance. I was reminded of how hard she had worked all week.

I jumped up and walked over to her. "Corinne, you know that fudge? I stole it. Or, I mean, I took it."

"What? My fudge?"

"Yes, but Marlena wouldn't let me eat it and she threw it out."

"You took my fudge?"

"Yes, I'm sorry. I apologize. That's why I bought you the cheesecake. I was too embarrassed ..."

She laughed. "It's just fudge, David." She hugged me and said, "You're forgiven."

As she walked back to rehearsal, she turned and said, "You know, I've done the same thing myself."

I knew we were kindred spirits. Fudge lovers.

On Saturday, on the plane home, Marlena told me she had returned the fudge to the freezer before we left. I was surprised by her duplicity. *Maybe it will still be there next summer,* I thought.

How I Spent
My Christmas
Vacation

Dear friends and family,

Medical update: The vascular malformation affecting the left side of my face, neck and head has slowly grown over my lifetime. In the last couple of years, my eating, speaking, breathing and sleeping have been significantly affected and I have had some discomfort and pain. I now have the opportunity to do something about it.

Dr. Chris Dowd, an eminent interventional radiologist at the University of California at San Francisco (UCSF) Medical Center, will identify, via fluoroscopy, enlarged vascular areas in my airway and mouth. He will inject a sclerosing agent that will cause the affected area to scar up, die, and be resorbed into the body. That, very briefly, is sclerotherapy. It is a simple procedure but one that has to be done carefully. The procedure will be performed on December twenty-first. Yes, I will most likely be in the ICU on Christmas Day. I plan to be as Tiny Tim-ishly inspirational as possible.

Bed Report:
I have acquired an adjustable bed and mastered the John Merrick/Elephant Man technique of sleeping in a quasi-upright position. I get large chunks of pain-free, solid sleep!

My prayer:
I pray that my life force and my immune system remain strong; my being accepts the procedures well, including the needles, dye and sclerosing agents; there is minimal swelling, bleeding and pain; those who care for me are fully present and operating at their highest skill level; I recuperate rapidly and continue my work in the world with greater efficiency, strength and heart. And oh yes, I really, really want to have a cute little pink tongue.

What I need from you:
Laughter, beauty, touch, prayer, music.
Flowers, especially roses. I favour Sterling, Lavande or American Beauty roses. Also, anything peach coloured.
Forgiveness. I am not sure what for. Just tell me that you forgive me.
With much appreciation and love,
David

December 21, 2001, 11:45 a.m.
I lie shivering on a gurney in the pre-op room of UCSF's Long Hospital. Marlena and our friend Terri barely fit into my little curtained cubicle. Marlena holds my hand. The pre-op room is composed of a dozen of these small, pseudo-private enclosures, each holding someone like me. The constant chatter of anesthesiologists and hospital staff prepping us

for surgery is disorienting. I am on some kind of med and I can't tell whether they are talking to me or someone else. I am beginning the familiar process of dissociation in the face of impending surgery. My feet are cold; I am afraid they will stay that way forever. My body tenses; I am afraid I will have needles imbedded in me for the rest of my life. Terri, the queen of advocates, finds an extra blanket for me.

December 21, afternoon
Just as I enter the operating room, the sun reaches its apogee, pauses for an extra tick and turns to ratchet north again. Winter solstice. A perfect day and a perfect time for surgery. Here comes the sun.

Under general anesthetic, I receive eleven separate injections of 70 percent ethanol, 30 percent dye directly into blood vessels in my tongue, airway and other parts of my lower cranium. It is designed to destroy many of the swollen, entangled blood vessels that are constricting my airway. Pretty toxic stuff. I have imbibed larger quantities of alcohol, albeit not directly into my bloodstream.

December 21, 9:00 p.m.
"Mr. Roche. Mr. Roche." I wake up in the Neurology Intensive Care Unit on the eleventh floor. Marlena and our friend Jo Anne enter my field of vision long enough for me to see that they are smiling. Real smiles. The kind that tell me things are okay.

I close my eyes and internally assess my body. I am pleased to find that I am not in pain.

In a morphine-induced mindfulness meditation, I observe that my bare right leg is poking out from under the blanket. I observe that a Foley catheter is taped to the inside of my right thigh. I observe that I don't have any pants on. I remember I had pants when I went into surgery. I miss those pants. Their soft, thin cotton material. The pattern that matched my gown. The lovely, dependable drawstring. They were baggy, but they were mine. While they were in my life, I loved them. I loved the sense of security and dignity they offered. How did those lovely pants come off? Did I take them off? Who took my pants off? Did they take them off as soon as I went under? Where are they? Oh well. I observe myself missing my pants, but not enough to do anything about it. Not right now. I slip away into a state of semi-torpor.

I awaken again and anchor on Marlena and Jo Anne. I can't speak. All I can do is absorb their presence.

December 22

My brother Patrick has arrived from San Diego. He looks handsome sitting next to Marlena. Marlena is beautiful. I can count on them. I am glad they are alive. I am glad Patrick is safe. He is saying something to Marlena. He talks so fast I can't understand, but I know it's funny because she is laughing.

December 23

My daughter Amy is here from Indiana. She looks thin. Her face glows. I am glad she is safe. I can count on her.

On my pad, I list what I want for bedtime. Socks. Blanket. Ambien. Marlena will tell it all to the nurse.

I like the ICU. The nurses are kind. They will do anything for me. My tongue, my airway, my soft palate—all are so swollen that I cannot talk. I use a very primitive American Sign Language, pointing to the light and grunting to get it turned on or off, or waving the door closed. At night, Nurse Carol fixes my pillows and tucks in my blankie around my feet to keep them warm. I deserve to be tucked in. The morphine makes it extra pleasant.

Marlena is always here. I want her warm hand. Any touch from her courses through me. She reads; she says prayers. Sometimes she looks worried. Her face is drawn, set, resolute.

December 23

I am happy—very happy—to report that hospitals have developed a better understanding of exactly why God created morphine. They are no longer so concerned about addiction. I hold what looks like a call button firmly in my left hand. But it does not call the nurse. It calls the morphine. Nurse James told me, "Press this every ten minutes and you get one milligram of morphine in your iv." Great! Good plan! I am on morphine and have a very dim sense of the passage of time. But I do have a strong, clear desire to get my full share of morphine. So I press that button every time I think about it, just in case ten minutes has already passed.

Nurse James returns. "How's your pain control, Mr. Roche?" He looks at the display. "Oh my. You pressed the button thirty-four times in the last hour. Are you having a lot of pain?" I am amused by his question. I observe myself slowly shaking my head no. For a moment I simply enjoy the sensation of my head moving from side to side. Then I come more or less back into the present. I press the red button again. Twice. Just to be sure.

December 23

The Neuro Intensive Care Unit is a timeless place. When a new nurse enters my room, I know it is either 7:00 a.m. or 7:00 p.m.—shift change. Other than that, it is hard to tell.

99

After a couple of days, the routines that mark time become clearer. It is like watching a nature film. "Here, on the vast Serengeti, the elephants come to the watering hole well before dawn. But the sun is high in the sky before the zebras get to the precious liquid."

Here, in my less-vast ICU room, dawn is signalled by a perfunctory quick knock at my door and arrives abruptly in the form of a fluorescent glare from the hallway, backlighting shadowy dark figures. Sunrise on my little Serengeti. A small herd of doctors and residents trots in and surrounds my bed. There is only one female—typical for this species. They are all quite young, apparently just past adolescence. The alpha male assumes his position at the left side of my bed. "Good morning, Mr. Roche. You're looking good. Any questions?" I am about 15 percent conscious. I do have questions. But they are somewhere in my reptilian brain, just trudging into the limbic area. It will be a good half hour or so before they reach my cerebral cortex. Then, as quickly as they appeared, the herd is gone. My questions die aborning.

In this room, there are no windows to the outside world. The wall between me and the nurses' station is all glass. I am in an observation chamber. People stare in as if I were a newborn panda bear. Everyone who enters my little world is concerned about my welfare. The world revolves around me.

December 24, Christmas Eve

I was supposed to stay in the ICU for up to ten days, but after only three I am downgraded from the $7,000-per-day ICU to an ordinary $2,000-per-day room. Room L1422 has a TV and a view that includes the east end of Golden Gate Park as well as downtown San Francisco. It looks very beautiful in the rain.

There is no refrigerator or bar, but they do provide a cabinet well-stocked with free gauze, tape and vinyl gloves. The bed has a waterproof pad. All meals are room service.

I wake up to find Amy and Marlena decorating the new room with cards and flowers and photos.

My subpersona, the one that Terri has nicknamed Tidy Boy, faces my vulnerability by seeking to firmly establish a zone of tidiness around me. I like the blankets to be just so, the bed exactly parallel to the window, the tissues in the exact same spot on the bedside table. The illusion of control can be very healing.

December 25, Christmas Day

I am awakened by a chill in my left nostril. Food product has been flowing through the endogastric (NG) tube in my nose down into my stomach. Christmas breakfast is being served. Nurse Shannon has poured a can of Resource into one of the plastic bags hanging from my IV rack. On the label it claims to be "pure nutrition." The main ingredient in Resource is water; the second is corn syrup. I am glad I can't taste it.

Tidy Boy is enchanted by the concept of eating and sleeping simultaneously. So efficient. No dishes to wash.

December 25, evening

In the operating room, the surgeon had sutured the NG tube to the inside of my right nostril, just at the tip of my nose. The idea is to prevent me from pulling it out. Every time it is even slightly tweaked, or much worse, jerked, it causes intense pain.

I roll halfway onto my right side to begin urinating into the container. As I shift my position, my elbow rolls onto the NG tube. It feels like my nose is being torn off. I scream and slosh fresh pee all over myself and the bed. I jerk again and scream again. I lurch out of bed, crying helplessly.

Someone comes running into the room. I say "Pee! Pee!" but he does not understand. I turn the empty urinal upside down over the bed and shake it up and down. He smiles, nods understanding and begins to change the bed.

An aide comes in and gives me a sponge bath. There is actually no sponge. Instead she uses diaper-like things. They are disposable and packaged in plastic bags, allowing them to be heated in the microwave. Their artificial "fresh scent" smells worse than the urine.

December 26, early morning
I see Christmas cards on the windowsill and realize that Christmas Day has slipped by.

I want to please the doctors. I want to heal faster so they will approve of me, like me and admire me. I'm showing off, trying to be a good boy, a high achiever. A therapist friend once told me that under stress we tend to return to the values that were first inculcated in us. I am grateful to my family and the nuns for teaching me such valuable life skills.

Again, the herd of dawn stalkers bursts in. All along the side of my bed, shadowy figures move against the light. One turns toward the door and I see a face. Male, slightly built, shockingly young. He bends over me, his face obscured again. He wiggles the trach and I gag, panic and grab his arm to stop him. He turns to someone behind him. To my right, a voice, calm and soothing, "Good morning, Mr. Roche. We are going to change your trach now." Warm hands gently hold my arms. I turn toward the voice.

Fine, I think. I don't care. I won't even wake up. I have

learned to be passive, I can do passive, I can turn off any notion of caring. I am turned back to my left and something is being done to my throat. Suddenly I do care, because something is being forced into the hole in my throat. Pain cuts quickly through the morphine haze. Worse than pain is the terrible pressure on my larynx, the sensation of being strangled. I spasm up, resisting, but my shoulders are pinned. That voice: "This will be done in a few seconds, Mr. Roche." And incredibly, I give in to the reassurance and for a few nanoseconds I think they are done. Then something is being hammered into my throat. Once, twice, again. I gag and choke and try to scream but can't get it out. Then they're done and gone. I lie there stunned, with my throat throbbing. I touch my throat. There is still a trach there. A new one. The day begins.

December 26, late morning

Awakening from a nap, I review the trach-replacement episode. I consider the possibility that it was a healing experience because the same sort of thing happened to me when I was an infant in the hospital, only then it was precognitive and could only be kept in my body memory. Maybe being conscious now will release those old memories. I guess so. I hope so.

December 26, night

The man next door begins a constant inchoate moaning. "*Uuuunh. Uuuunh. Uuuunh.*" On and on. I am sympathetic, even though it keeps me awake. I wonder whether he is the unit's designated moaner. I wonder whether I have been moaning in my sleep. I begin to find a certain rhythm, a music in his moaning, so that it becomes white noise, and I drift in and out of sleep.

December 27

How are you feeling this morning? How are you feeling this afternoon? How are you feeling this evening? How are you feeling, Dad? How are you feeling, honey? How are you feeling, David? How are you feeling, Mr. Roche? How does your tongue feel? How does your throat feel? Let's have a look, shall we? How does that feel?

Can I have some more water? What are you going to do to me? When is Dr. Dowd going to be here? When is Dr. Murr going to be here? What's that in your hand? What's going to happen now? Another blanket, please? Would you close the door? Would you turn the light off? What is it like outside? What is that beeping noise? Why is that light blinking? What is that smell? When can I leave?

December 27, lunchtime

I have successfully swallowed a glass of water! Six ounces! I graduate to semi-solid food. It is still a painful effort to swallow. The food does not provide much incentive. The puréed carrots are the kind that are shipped and stored in fifty-gallon drums. The Jell-O has a distinct metallic taste. There is a tiny little paper napkin on the tray, just big enough to catch one good drool. I long for the good old days when I was fed through my nose.

After dinner I doze. I dream. It is 1956, and I am eating a hot lunch at the cafeteria of Our Lady of Grace School in Highland, Indiana. It is Wednesday, and the largest compartment in my metal lunch tray has peas and carrots with cubed Spam.

I awaken to find my friend John Malloy sitting at my bedside. Visitors have been restricted, but John is the type who simply arrives. I'm glad because he is not the type of visitor who takes my energy. In fact, the force of his personality fills the room and I can feed off it for a bit.

I have lost twelve pounds in one week while being fed through a tube. Hey! The Alternate Orifice Ingestion Diet! A money-making idea. TV infomercials! I envision myself effortlessly sliding an NG tube down the nose of a smiling model who is jabbering enthusiastically to an admiring studio audience. Clients would have to come in once a week to have their tubes changed and to purchase our special brand of nutrition supplement. I could call it Manna™. I'd have to figure out a way to make the NG tube into a fashion statement. Maybe they could come in different colours. The ones for men would be slightly larger. Maybe with the logos of sports teams. And why not the NG diet for your overweight dog or cat?

December 27, afternoon
The NG tube has been unstitched from my nose!

Friend Kathleena is giving me a foot rub. Friend Ginger is doing Feldenkrais bodywork on my left shoulder. Amy is sitting at my bedside, her hand on my knee, as she begins to read aloud the Morning Prayers that she and Marlena helped me to write.

"I let go and trust in God and my friends. I am supported by prayers and love from all over the world." Amy pauses, then repeats that sentence.

For the first time in the hospital, I let go. I sob and sob as Amy continues.

"My life force and immune system are strong. I accept my treatment well. There is just enough sclerosing and swelling for proper healing, no more, no less. Those who care for me are fully present and operating at their highest skill level."

As Amy reads each line, she stops and comments and encourages me. I weep for about twenty minutes, the most I have ever cried at one time in my entire life.

December 28, early morning
Dr. Ng comes in on rounds and tells me I will get out today. Good.

Everything about the hospital is repulsive. Everything stinks. The food. The room. The nurses. The sheets. My gown. Me. The waterproof pad in the bed has made me sweat and stink for days. My breath stinks. My trach gives off a fetid aroma. I roll out of bed. I sneak into the shower to wash myself off as best I can. The hot water is luxurious. I get dressed in the clothes I wore into the hospital. I go out of the room, down the hall to the public phone. I notice it is 6:45 a.m. I know Marlena will not be awake. I leave a wheezy message: "Hi, hon. It's me. I'm ready to go home. Come and get me." I go back to L1422. I make the bed. I sit in the chair. I wait. I refuse to return to the stinky bed. I wait till breakfast. I wait till lunch. I wait till the middle of the afternoon before I get angry at Marlena and Amy. Where the hell are they? How could they not come and get me right away?

December 28, 4:00 p.m.
Dr. Murr arrives. He has been out of town for the holidays, is stopping by to see how I am doing. I tell him I'm ready to go home now. He looks at my throat, at my trach. He says, "We might want to leave that trach open for a few months in case

we want to go in there again." The timing of his suggestion is not good.

December 28, 5:00 p.m.
Marlena and Amy arrive. They have taken a day off, been to get their hair done. They did not get my early message. They both look so good. I am so happy to see them that my anger about having to wait disappears.

December 28, evening
Home again. I am distressed to find that it smells the same as the hospital. It's then that I realize the smell is actually inside me. It is a byproduct of sclerotherapy. The toxins are still leaching out into my mouth and throat, and that is what smells.

I am arguing with Marlena and Amy. I don't know why. I want the house to be tidy. It is not tidy enough. I need to have that sense of order around me. My anger returns.

Amy intervenes. "Dad, you know Marlena has been really, really busy."

Half my voice comes through the trach, half is normal. The pain of talking does not keep me out of full rant mode.

"I need. Order. To heal. People say. I am strong. Yes. Healing good. Why? Tidy? Not anal. Neat! Not just control. Who I am. You make fun. I need. Order. Who I am. Who. I. Am."

Marlena and Amy stare, bewildered.

"Honey, don't use your energy for control. You need to relax, take care of yourself. This is a time for surrender."

"Surrender!?" I wheeze through the trach. "Never. Surrender. In my life. No. Surrender. Now."

"Dad, maybe you could think of it as letting go."

I remember how I let go and cried in the hospital. I start crying again, hysterically. I know they are right, but I don't know how to do surrender.

December 31
A chill Pacific storm brings the steady whap of rain against the windows of my room. It is a good time to be in bed recuperating.

My life has changed. From the sclerotherapy, yes, that's one of the ways. I already breathe and sleep better than I can ever remember.

I know I have changed in other ways, but I don't know how exactly. I know I have been living in a vortex of love. It has come in many different forms: prayers, good wishes, loving thoughts, chanting, expressions of support, calling upon ancestors, Hail Marys, smoke ceremonies, masses, meditations, candles lit, performances dedicated to me, songs sung for me, beauty of all sorts coming into my life.

I did not realize at first what was happening. The love and support that people sent me came first into the deepest parts of my self, into my unconscious. It appeared first in my dreams. The week before my surgery, a different dream came each night. The anxiety dreams that were a nightly staple of my dream diet were replaced by dreams of being loved and supported by many different people. Each night the sweetness of a new dream awoke me. I lay half awake in unaccustomed nighttime bliss six nights in a row. I could not ignore what was happening. And then in daily life, I slowly opened to the love that was coming to me.

January 2, 2002, via email

Dear friends and family,

Marlena and I offer warm, deep gratitude for all you have given us, most especially your prayers and good wishes. To be the recipient of such love has changed my life in ways that I can only dimly understand right now.

My dear daughter, Amy, who was here for most of my recuperation to date, has returned safely to Indiana.

This morning, otolaryngologist Dr. Andrew Murr did the first post-op evaluation and found I have made outstanding progress. The whole process of healing generally takes about six weeks, yet my airway is already clearer than it has been in my memory. (This is what your support did!)

Dr. Murr put a cap on the trach (yay!). I will be admitted again to the hospital on Tues., Jan. 8, when Dr. Murr will remove the trach entirely (YAY!). I will stay for twenty-four-hour observation and be discharged to celebrate my fifty-eighth birthday on January 9th!

Of course, I am still quite swollen, and my tongue feels like sandpapered roadkill. But overall, things have gone very well, and I can safely say I am over the hump.

Throughout January, I will still be incommunicado, needing to rest, recuperate and develop my inner life. I do promise to write you at more length about the whole process in a way that may be helpful to others (as well as funny).

Because the notion of having alcohol injected directly into one's head is, to me, inherently funny.

Lots of love,

David

Master Storytellers

A bank of windows overlooks the Malaspina Strait on an overcast day in the rainforest. Marlena and I are in a conference room in Powell River, BC.

The occasion: a storytelling workshop for people with developmental and other disabilities sponsored by the Powell River Association for Community Living (PRACL). There are about two dozen attendees.

Marlena and I, the facilitators, introduce ourselves. I talk about my facial difference, wanting simply to get it out of the way. No one seems interested.

I begin to explain that this is a storytelling event but before I get out the second sentence, two people get up from their chairs to tell stories.

First is Bill. A white man, he looks to be in his sixties. He stands to my right and begins talking, looking right at me. I point him toward the audience. I can only understand a fraction of what he says. But his voice is intimate, and he has great gestures. His persona comes through; everyone else seems to understand him.

He may have been talking about wood carving because one person gives feedback about Bill's great walking sticks. This launches him again; I catch the phrase *wood burning*.

As Bill is sitting down, Ty heads toward the front. He is thirty-six years old, about three feet tall, with severe scoliosis. His mother, Lucy, announces from the audience that he is legally blind and is deaf in one ear. As Lucy talks, Ty repeats, "Yeah, yeah, yeah, yeah, yeah, yeah, yeah." When Ty begins to speak, within fifteen seconds Lucy gets up from her chair and announces she is going to help him. Putting Ty on her lap, she says he is "seventy pounds of cute trouble." She describes Ty's family history and how he had come to live with her and her husband, how his biological father had visited but there was "no bonding." Ty fidgets and starts listing his friends and what he does with them: bowling with Ken, watching movies with Matt, adding up to about a dozen friends and activities. He ends by singing "You Are My Sunshine."

Then dapper Patrick comes up, dressed like a Vancouver dandy, with a leather coat and an *au courant* grey goatee. He talks about his mother's death, how he is still grieving, how he gets depressed. Around the circle, heads nod.

After each story we ask for appreciation for the story just told, but that is not what we get. Instead, people are told how appreciated they are as people, as members of the community. "Do you remember when you got all gutter balls?" "Yeah," with an abashed expression that brings a lot of laughter.

Margaret comes up with Calum, who works at PRACL. Margaret, in her thirties, with a round face and beautiful black hair, is deaf and also cannot speak. She had pasted pictures in a scrapbook and John interprets them for her. "Margaret loves to read. She loves her cats." As he speaks, he signs for Margaret. Her face shines out at the others; she looks as lovely as anyone at the Oscars.

Matt and Ken and Bill inspire each other. All three of them are in John's communications class. It is difficult for me to understand much of what they say, but the others are fully with them. Their desire to communicate and connect is so powerful that it has overcome verbal difficulties. They sign as they talk, their bodies and faces so expressive that they seem to full-body dance their stories. Marlena tells Matt his speaking reflects a good sense of himself.

During the coffee break, John explains to me that they all had studied actors on TV and in the movies and learned from them nuances of physical expression.

After the break, I ask whether anyone wants to come up and receive appreciation even if they are too shy to tell a story. Brian, who wears a heavy-metal t-shirt, immediately announces, "No way," but everyone ignores him. Victor likes the idea but will not go up without his friend Jane. They sit in chairs in front of the group. They are a little confused about what to do until Marlena says, "Just take the love into your hearts."

Victor says, "Oh, I can do that." They look out together and for several moments simply absorb the wonderful strength of the community.

As the afternoon goes on, I start to realize they all know how to recognize and acknowledge inner beauty. And show it. Any pronouncements from me would be completely redundant.

Marlena and I have done many storytelling workshops with people with disabilities. We are used to how they build community, and we admire it. On this day, every story is about exaltation of and exultation in community. The storytellers, each in their own way, show superior abilities in matters of the heart, in the understanding of what it means to be a human being, in the vulnerability of being human.

Brian is in his early twenties. He has few teeth and is a consistently vocal, negative presence. If he does not understand what someone is saying, he announces it: "What? What? What is he saying?" He points to the floor and loudly proclaims, "I worship the god below." I am a little wary when he wants to come up. He asks Gord to stand with him and then does imitations of the Tasmanian Devil, Achmed the Dead Terrorist and Bugs Bunny.

Janet is tall, with black hair, fair skin and clear blue eyes. She tells a remarkable story of achieving her life dream of climbing Mount Kilimanjaro.

People are definitely impressed by her climb of Kilimanjaro, but they are just as impressed by Brian's Bugs Bunny impression, Ty's singing and Victor's willingness to simply accept love. Love is the currency. Sort of like an early version of Bitcoin. Lovecoin.

My Name Is Marie

"My name is Marie. I'm from Prince Rupert. I'm from the Musqueam Nation."

She is about five-foot-two, with drab clothing, a round face, bad teeth. I use the term "bad teeth" advisedly. Most everyone here in this room has bad teeth (including me). I don't have any teeth at all except for store-bought ones that rent my mouth space during the day. In Marin County, California, where I used to live, everyone had glistening, even white teeth, so white that sometimes I felt as if I was in a *Twilight Zone* episode. Most people would not go out of the house if they had a missing tooth. But not here in the Vancouver Drug Users Resource Centre on Cordova Street in the Downtown Eastside (DTES).

Marie has a "stand and deliver" storytelling style. Her story is short and to the point. From the interior of BC to the DTES at age eleven. From poverty there to poverty here. To drugs, alcohol and working the streets.

She says she is doing very well but not totally clean and sober. I love that she does not claim to be clean and sober. She realized she did not want to keep on using and drinking when she saw what it did to other women. She imitates a woman lying on the sidewalk, babbling and waving her arms; it's not a full-blown take but powerful enough to bring the street woman into the room with us. Marie returns to being herself, and she is an advocate. She talks to these women on the street, she tells them about services and brings them to the women's shelter.

Her story is a familiar one. Her story is her self, her presence. Her stand. Her honesty.

I recognize her beauty. What shines in her also shines out. I can see her soul. I have learned how to do that. I am a story encourager, a story *eliciter*, a story nurturer, a story lover. Love your story, love you, see your beauty, love your beauty. You and your story, both irresistible.

I recognize what Marie is doing because I do that. It took me a long time, but I found out that what people want most from me on stage is to be myself.

When Marie speaks, I hear the voice of the soul. I hear hope. Perhaps that is idealistic, naive of me, but I can only recognize and claim and proclaim my own experience. Step by step, slowly, slowly, Marie and all of us are trying to discover who we are. Her journey is a hero's journey. Telling stories is part of that process.

What good does it do to tell your story and claim your humanity? For one thing, it radiates outward to others. Other people see and hear you doing that, and they start to believe it is possible for them too.

George gets up, an Elder without a place to be an Elder.

He is from the residential school system. He got to fourth grade without speaking English. He spoke Latin before he spoke English because he read the Bible in Latin. "They put me with the 'retards,'" he says. Then he got his degree from UC Berkeley.

Then Kennedy, a former Sunshine Coast resident in her thirties (with good teeth!) and a strong upper body that gives evidence of her physical work as a plumber. She begins by identifying herself as being of Portuguese heritage and queer, with the latter being important to her because it is her choice.

Next is Earl, a writer, a poet. He writes poetry in his language and translates it to young people from his band. His examples are powerful.

Tia Maria is from the north woods of Ontario, one of eleven children. Her father was a trapper who built a log-cabin house with the logs vertical. She knows how to trap, to hunt, to live off the land. Now she knows how to live on the DTES.

I love this storytelling, I love hearing and bringing out and validating voices that need to be heard.

The voices of women. The voices of people with disabilities. Indigenous voices. I want them all to be heard.

What difference does it make? I don't know—I just know I have this calling. I am being drawn away from the stage to being a story lover, encourager, nurturer—a story empowerer.

At the Carnegie Centre

In Vancouver, BC, I walk the twelve blocks down Hastings Street from Burrard to Main, on my way to perform at the Carnegie Centre. I am journeying from the business and convention hub of the city to the Downtown Eastside, from individualism and striving for dominance toward striving for survival and the recognition of common humanity. I will be giving a performance of my signature solo show, "The Church of 80% Sincerity."

Along the way, the storefronts segue from upscale boutiques, pubs, galleries and chocolatiers to head shops and surplus stores. Then vacant lots, graffiti, an occasional art gallery. Why are there vacant lots near downtown Vancouver? They must be owned by developers; before long, the cranes that dominate the rest of downtown will be slow dancing above these mean streets.

The fence in front of a construction site has a large billboard proclaiming the soon-to-be existence of Seaview Towers, and it says that now is the time to buy the condos that will exist there next year. I wonder who has the confidence to purchase a space in the air? I wonder who feels that a space in the air can belong to anyone?

I walk close to the curb and away from the doorways even though it is light out. I still hold memories of being assaulted on the street. I realize I am living in my past experience and begin to relax into the moment instead.

A few minutes ago on Burrard Street, a young woman with an expensive haircut and a nicely tailored suit talked happily on her iPhone on the way home from her office. Now, seven blocks farther along, a young woman, gaunt, with ragged jeans and a dirty t-shirt, straggly hair and multiple tattoos on bare arms, talks into space with no iPhone to pick up her conversation.

Buildings change from having edges and corners and glass and impossible height to being lower and closer to the ground, and looking older, warmer and more attractive, more accessible, with an almost grandmotherly ambience.

I have crossed Vancouver's invisible line. Now it's okay for people to sit or lie down on the sidewalk, to relax there (or to fidget or pace), to hang out with friends and smoke, to panhandle, to enjoy the sun when it peeks through. This is Vancouver's commons. I am more in the mix of people now and something softens inside me. I can smell people, and I like that. Even when the smells are a little rank, they are strangely comforting. I am reminded of my brother Kevin peeing in bed every night. Even now, the smell of stale urine makes me miss him.

A man comes up to me holding an unlit cigarette in the palm of his hand. "Loonie," he says with an inquiring and oddly earnest look.

"No, thank you." I am dressed casually but I don't think I look like I belong here. Then I remember that my facial difference is my passport. I have membership privileges here. His breath reeks from three feet away. I am jarred for a moment but remember the medication on the breath of men dying of AIDS in San Francisco, that almost omnipresent smell, and the scent of shit in their diapers and how even that became so familiar and somehow acceptable. Here again I am in the company of people who are more familiar with death, and I recall how, back then, in the epidemic, dying people stripped away so many of my illusions and the stories I had chosen to live out for so many years. This is good preparation for my performing.

Ten blocks back, along Burrard, people walked briskly, heading somewhere, with a goal. They clumped together only when waiting to cross intersections or at bus stops, where they tended to stare blankly ahead or at the ground, many with earbuds that locked the outside world away. Here, closer to Main, people saunter and meander, not going anywhere special. This is where they are, where they belong. They are very aware of each other, they greet each other. When I make eye contact, they nod hello. I become less of an observer, more of a participant. My breath deepens. This is a culture change.

I arrive at the pre-event dinner sponsored by an agency that helps unemployed people find jobs. A couple of dozen people are milling around the food table. I am reminded of old Jewish ladies observing and commenting on the food laid out after the bar mitzvah as they position themselves to get to the best choices. Here there are two choices of lasagna: meat or veggie. Both are gooey, and I cannot eat them before performing. I stuff two oatmeal raisin cookies and a bottle of Minute Maid orange juice into my bag for after the show.

During dinner, people introduce themselves. They are supposed to say who they are and what they would like from the evening.

Roderick wants humour. Okay, I can do that.

Lise is a traffic control person, a flag lady. She thanks the agency for finding her a job and for helping her get gear.

They want to hear about me. I feel I have to go deep with these folks. I tell how I gained the confidence to be a performer by sharing at AA meetings.

All together, we troop up Main to the Carnegie Centre, where a mass of people is out on the sidewalk. It's like the Tenderloin neighbourhood in San Francisco, like outside Glide Memorial Church on a Sunday morning. Bodies wasted, shrivelled, bloated, tattooed, scarred, bent over into a permanent cringe. No makeup, no fancy clothing, no moisturizer, no Fluevog shoes, no rows of even white teeth. Outer façades have been stripped away, leaving only raw soul. There are occasional outbursts from those souls. Mostly people seem to just want to be together. These are social animals; this seems natural, this seems like our basic nature, this is where we belong. What is this comfort we take in one another?

I have stepped into this way of being. I like it here, I am tuned in to the crowd, I start behaving like them, very aware of other people, who they are. Is it like an AA meeting, where a group of people who are all aware they are deeply flawed is willing to sit together and respect, listen to and love each other for an hour.

It's so much easier to be with people without pretense. I realize this is where I thrive, in intimacy, and I am going to be creative in a few moments. I breathe into my chakras, I feel it is all going to be okay. I am already feeding off my audience.

Inside, I find a surprisingly large audience, warm and engaged and present. I am on stage in bright, warm light, with amplification, and that usually means a sort of fourth wall. I have asked that the house lights be up halfway so I can see the audience, look into their eyes. As I perform, I can feel them. I feed them, they feed me. It's not an audience, it's more of a street crowd. I keep my hands open toward them; I can feel their energy.

What is it that I do on stage? I am just being myself. Yes to funny, yes to warm funny, yes to authenticity. I tell stories that are sweet, funny, dark, painful, any combination thereof. What is really happening is that I am revealing myself. In about ten minutes I have shape-shifted from someone with a facial disfigurement into someone incredibly beautiful. This is what they want and need and love, and so do I.

After my show, lots of people want to talk. Many just come up to say thanks or give and get hugs.

Shirley says, "My boyfriend told me I was fat and ugly and that I better stay with him, so I stayed with him for twenty years. I came to Vancouver from residential school. I always feel like people are making fun of me. Some bad things have happened to me."

Lydia says, "I used down here many years ago myself, so I know what it is like. Let me tell you, things change very slowly down here. But they do change. Thirty years I have been working here. The last ten years, there have been things changing that are not just Band-Aids. This project that works with people and businesses who are here, this is one example."

Lazslo says, "Have you read Alan Watts? I've been reading him lately."

Mike says, "I got a job at the Olympic Village. I hated it. I had to lean out from my ladder. I had restraints on, but I was scared. They told me I was not doing what I was told. So I got a different job."

Mike wins the door prize of a copy of my book by being the first person able to say where I live. "Yeah, this will be the first book I ever read in my life."

Roberto says, "I hated my job for a year but now I like it."

Carol Ann asks, "What do you tell people when they ask you about being short?"

Roderick comes up and covers his mouth when he talks. "I had a friend who died of AIDS. It took a long time. He was in hospice, then he came out, then in palliative care. He was in Saint Paul's. I saw him just about every day. People tried to console me when he died, but I was not there for him. I was in his room, then I went down on the street to buy something and I was out all night, and when I got back he was dead. So, I was not there for him."

I feel fully accepted into this community. Out on the street again afterward, I linger, soaking in the humanity around me, looking at everyone with new eyes, hearing more, feeling at one with where I am and who I am with.

Two Months to the Day

May 10, 2016

Dear Family,

It has been two months to the day since I stepped off the plane in San Francisco with a urinary tract infection that, two hours later, had me in the emergency room of St. Luke's Hospital, unconscious, with a heart rate of 160 and a temperature of 104. I had arrived at the home of my friends Kenneth and Carmen Barnes. Ken is a physician who took me to the ER within a few minutes of my arriving at their house. If I had been home in Roberts Creek, I'd have decided I just needed to go to bed—and would not have awakened.

So I award myself ten points for being alive. And fifteen points for having Ken as a friend. Total of twenty-five so far.

I have been followed up thoroughly here at home in British Columbia—my heart, my bladder, prostate, mental state. My psychiatrist, Marius Welgemoed (he's such a nice guy; I had never been to a psychiatrist before and was a little nervous), told me it can take up to a year for the brain to fully recover from delirium. I have been feeling basically fine but still a beat or two behind mentally and physically. He gave me a cognition test, on which I did well. I was proudest of the fact that he read five words to me and I had to repeat them. Okay, no big problem. But then a few minutes later I had to repeat them *again*. Whoa! But I did it! Wow. Ten points for that. Makes thirty-five. And twenty-five more points for Canadian health care! Sixty!

Marlena has me on an anti-inflammatory diet, which basically means no gluten, sugar or dairy. No miraculous results after the first week, but I am doing it. Pretty amazing considering the first meal of my entire life consisted of evaporated milk and corn syrup. Interestingly, that was considered much healthier than breast milk in 1944. Apparently I liked it! Minus five points for the anti-inflammatory diet because I really like sweet, doughy fried things. Total is now holding at fifty-five. We are coming down to the finish line with the *Love at Second Sight* video. The theme song just got out of studio, and let me tell you, it is fantastic. I hope I get to share it with you soon. I think it will go viral. Twenty points for finishing excellent song but minus five for inappropriate self-confidence. Total: seventy.

We are planning two premieres so far. One in Vancouver at the Simon Fraser University at Woodward's Cinema. A 350-seat theatre! Why not? (See where inappropriate self-confidence can lead a person?) The other will be in Mill Valley. Both in September. Premieres are five points for the first one, two for fifteen. Total: eighty-five.

And, *mirabile dictu* (you can look that up; it's one of the useful phrases I learned in the seminary), I have a good shot at a big role in a feature film. The director is Alexandre Franchi; he's legit—one of his films got best Canadian feature at the Toronto International Film Festival. It's set in a support group for people with facial differences. We are planning to take over the world (just kidding). I'll have to do a screen test soon. If I get it, we shoot in Montreal in the winter. Five points for using Latin phrase. Total: ninety.

Marlena is running on all eighteen cylinders. (What, you didn't know she had that many cylinders? She does indeed.) I drag her out into the garden sometimes. Her favourite activity is going to the memory care centre in Gibsons and hanging out with people who are totally in the moment. She always seems happy, and I like that because I am more dour than she is but am a happiness parasite, feeding off her. Ten points for successful parasitism. That's one hundred!

What else? You tell me. Got any questions?

Warmest and confidentest and parasitest,

David

Love at Second Sight

Moment of Grace 1: The Birth of *Love at Second Sight*

The concept for *Love at Second Sight* began in Vancouver, British Columbia, in 1998. I had been hired to do the opening keynote at the conference of the Foundation for Nager and Miller Syndromes. These syndromes, present at birth, affect appearance radically. The foundation, founded by the amazing Margaret Hogan, offers support for families of children with these syndromes.

By that point in our marriage, Marlena had little interest in travelling to hear me speak. She'd say, "I'll travel to the kitchen. That's about it." But beautiful Vancouver and a couple of getaway days lured her. We were guests at the pre-conference dinner on Friday evening. Children with all sorts of physical anomalies ran or were wheeled around, excited and playful, filled with happiness and light. Marlena was completely charmed and fell in love, especially with five-year-old Syrus.

The next morning I awoke at 6:00, mentally and emotionally preparing myself. Somehow, suddenly it seemed the most natural thing in the world for Marlena to give the keynote with me. I did not have a plan, I just wanted her to do it. I shook her awake. "Honey, I want you to do the keynote with me." I had her at a disadvantage because she is a night person and usually would never be awake at that hour. Several expressions flashed across her sleepy face before she answered yes.

It is highly unusual for a keynote speaker to share the podium with a spouse, especially without notice. But I felt no doubts, and Margaret agreed. I have no memory of Marlena and me planning what she was going to say.

I spoke for about fifteen minutes and then introduced her. She stepped to the podium and looked out at two hundred people. She paused, breathed them in and began: "The first time I met David I did not see his face. I heard his voice." And she went on to describe her shock and revulsion when she did see me. She described the confusion and shame she had felt as she walked away from me.

The audience was rapt as she told of sorting through her feelings that day and finally following her heart back to me. It was the first time she had ever told that story. Her last line, coming after the kind of wonderful storytelling pause when you can observe the storyteller searching her insides, waiting for the feelings to rise and become words and come out into the world, was "You know ... I think I saw David's soul."

The audience did not applaud. They sat there, semi-stunned. Tears flowed from the parents' eyes. They did not want this to end. That last sentence washed over the room. Not only the sentence—it was simply the holder for the *feeling*, which was not just Marlena's feeling but a feeling that belonged to everyone in the audience, especially those who had had the experience of seeing their child's soul. Marlena was validating their experience as well as showing them that it was not theirs alone, but universal.

What Marlena had done was the essence of great story-telling. She was a time machine, simultaneously present in the past and the now. She was dwelling in her own soul as it brought the full meaning of the past into the room for the listeners to take into their own souls.

And so, *Love at Second Sight* was born in truth and love, launched in that exquisite moment of grace. In that simple sentence, Marlena had compressed life stories into a few seconds charged with meaning and love and what it meant to truly see another human being.

That feeling, that energy filled the room. Everyone, joined together by that one sentence, felt the deepest part of what it meant to be a human being, to truly love. We all were steeped in that for a moment, into a place of wordless love.

It was time for the breakout sessions, but everyone was in a timeless, still place. In the audience, a woman rose from her seat. A woman of the earth, a solid woman, a midwife named Irena. She did not identify herself by name; she simply began her story.

She told of being present at the birth of Patrick, who, just moments after his birth, was taken and set on a metal tray. Irena realized that Patrick was either stillborn or being left to die. His leg twitched; Irena immediately picked him up. His mother lifted her head, saw Patrick and cried out for her child. Irena put him in her arms. No one spoke. Irena summoned a priest, who anointed Patrick and gave him the last rites. He never cried, for he had been born without lungs, with no ability to breathe. His movement slowed. He shuddered and passed away in his mother's arms.

Irena said, "Patrick only lived for a few minutes. Yet every second of his life was filled with love. Who among us can claim that for ourselves? What a wonderfully blessed life he led."

Moment of Grace 2: Grace and Grief

At the Marin Country Day School Beyond-Borders program, we presented in their cozy black-box theatre. During question-and-answer period, we were talking about teasing. Marlena imitated a person talking with a hand cupped over her mouth while stealing looks at someone else who was the topic of the hidden conversation. She was offering this as an example of an activity that could be interpreted as teasing even when it wasn't intended as such. After we were done, a girl came up to Marlena. As she came closer, she broke into sobs. Marlena took her in her arms. The girl tried to talk but couldn't get the words out because of the depth of her sorrow. Her girlfriends approached and surrounded her, and they explained that her father had died over the summer.

The other students did not know how to deal with this death. Eventually it came out she had often experienced them talking about her behind their hands. She had sometimes felt that everyone was staring at her, everyone was gossiping about her. Marlena's example had triggered her memories of that and her grief, and she was expressing it in public for the first time. Her friends began stroking her arms, shoulders, back and hands, and a couple of them began to brush her hair. Her healing was born in that moment of grace.

Moment of Grace 3: Grace and the Revelation of Friendship

At White Hill School, in Marin County, California, during the question-and-answer session, Marlena asked the students whether they had ever taken a second look at anyone. This question was unplanned, and it was a little alarming to me when she invited a boy to the front of the room and gave him the microphone. I was on alert to retrieve the mic when Andrew, facing Marlena, began his story.

"Well, when I saw Jose, I noticed the way he looked, which was very different, but I decided to get to know him and now we're good friends."

Students began to applaud but Marlena held her palm up to shush them. Looking into the audience at a grinning boy, she said, "Are you Jose?" Without prompting, Jose came up to join her and Andrew. He had what appeared to be a cleft lip and a limp that gave him a rolling gait but did not prevent him from being kind of strutty. Andrew handed him the mic.

Jose turned to the audience. "My mother was nervous about me coming to a new school. But I feel good about myself." Jose threw his arm around Andrew and they both smiled.

Along the wall and in back, teachers and counsellors were weeping, and that moment of grace washed over them and two hundred students.

Moment of Grace 4: Grace and the Discovery of Love

I saw Karen at a benefit in Vancouver. She lit up when she saw me, and she wheeled up and began talking.

"I have a great story for you. I went to your *Love at Second Sight* premiere at the Simon Fraser Woodward's Cinema in

September. Of course I loved it, of course I cried. But you know what? I had been seeing this guy for a couple of years, on and off. Off and on, really. He was just not good for me. Then there was this other guy who kept asking me out. But I kept letting him slide away. After I saw *Love at Second Sight,* I decided to give him a second look, just like Marlena says."

There he was, standing beside her.

Her moment of grace had brought a second look, a change of heart, and love.

Moment of Grace 5: Grace and Community

Marlena and I were presenting *Love at Second Sight* at Saint Isabella School in Terra Linda, California. It is a Catholic school with strong community values.

During the part where Marlena describes moving from a school with three hundred students to being the new girl at a school of four thousand and the challenges that come with that, I noticed a girl off to our right covering her face and weeping.

I went to Marlena and pointed her out. Marlena hesitated, stopped talking, walked over to the student and waited. It turned out that the girl was new in school and felt shy. Marlena's story about her own new school had stirred her. Other kids and teachers came around her, forming a small community of comfort. Marlena stepped back to the front of the class, gave a small honouring nod to that group, and continued her story.

That moment of grace had brought that young girl more fully into a loving community.

Moment of Grace 6: The Flow of Grace

Marlena and I arrived early at Mill Valley Middle School, in the town where we'd previously lived north of San Francisco, for a presentation of our video. We looked for our friend Anna Lazzarini, the principal, to say hello and get a hug. She was on duty on the playground, so we headed out past the staff room into the lunchtime sun. We found Anna and chatted briefly; she had to keep her attention on the students.

A tall, stocky boy came and stood about six feet away from us. He was staring at me but with little visible emotion. As we turned to go back into the school, he stepped in front of me and said, "Hey, you are so ugly."

Because he presented his perspective as a simple statement of fact, without verbalized malice, I simply accepted what he said and replied, "Well, actually, I am not ugly. I am unique."

He answered, "No, you are ugly."

We said nothing and continued on into the school.

After our live presentation to a room full of Grade 6 students, we took questions and comments. This was always the most enjoyable part for us.

A boy said, "You know? It's interesting. It's awesome that human beings have the ability to take a second look at someone."

Sitting immediately in front of him, a girl exulted and bounced up. "After I saw this film, I just ... I just feel happy. Really, really, really happy. I don't know why. I just do."

The boy who saw me as ugly was sitting off to the side of the other students. An adult was with him. When the bell rang, he stepped up to me and Marlena and said, "You're handsome. You're really cool." He turned and left.

I counted three moments of grace there: the remarkable comment from the first boy, the joy of the bouncing girl, and the compliment from the boy who had said twice that I was ugly.

Moment of Grace 7: Grace Empowers

Elizabeth Grumbach, a teacher at Moses Brown School in Providence, Rhode Island, had heard about me and checked out my website. She found an interview I had done with CNN, streamed it for her Grade 6 students and then Skyped me in to do a Q&A. The first question was: "When did you see the light inside yourself?"

It shook and thrilled me to have a young person ask such a question. Moses Brown is a Quaker school with a strong emphasis on character development; they strive to have each other see the inner light in everyone. What a wonderful way to build diversity and community!

I tried my best to answer that question by saying that the light was already inside me when I was born and that my family saw and fed it so that, although at many points in my life I forgot that light, it was always there. I could always find a way to see it, and most of the time that was because family or friends reminded me it was there.

A few weeks afterward, Elizabeth emailed to let me know that two of her students had been so excited by the Skyping session that they wanted to bring me to Moses Brown School in person. They had gone to the head of the school and received the go-ahead to make that happen. They held a lemonade-stand fundraiser and raised $600 toward bringing Marlena and me across the continent from British Columbia to Rhode Island.

The two girls met us at the entrance to the school, showed us around and introduced us at two different presentations. We could tell they were a little nervous when they introduced us to the other high schoolers, but in spite of that they were entirely present and confident. Their inner light was shining. They had seized a moment of grace and made it blossom.

Now, when I awaken in the morning, I turn on my inner light. I try to let it shine and I carry its message forward.

Moment of Grace 8: The Grace of Friendship

We were at a small middle school in a rural area on the northern coast of California. The room held only about fifty students. Marlena asked whether any of them had ever had anyone take a second look at them.

It is helpful to have someone lead by example in answering such a question. In such a relatively small community, it is not unusual to watch the students turn to someone they want to take the lead and answer. And there she was, a person of colour, tall with the girl height common at that age. She stood up almost immediately.

"Well, this isn't a second look, exactly. But anyway, I'm on the basketball team and we were playing San Geronimo in their gym. Some of the San Geronimo kids started calling me names. Like the n-word, a lot. I could hear them, especially when I was running by. I was getting upset and mad too. So I stopped and was just standing there and my teammates, I guess they heard it too ..."

"We did," said two other girls.

"They just came up and stood by me. They didn't say anything."

"We stared them down."

"Yeah, we stared them down."

"It was so cool."

That was it. She sat down after offering a healthy serving of grace to us all.

Moment of Grace 9: Grace Affirmed

At Preston Middle School in Fort Collins, Colorado, Marlena and I did an evening presentation for parents after being with the students in the afternoon. This was our second year in a row at Preston.

A teacher came up to thank us. In a surprising moment of doubt, Marlena said, "Sometimes I wonder if it's worth it."

The teacher looked shocked. "Oh no, no. The girls talk about this all the time."

A nice moment of grace delivered directly to Marlena.

Moment of Grace 10: Paying Grace Forward

In my signature solo show, "The Church of 80% Sincerity," I would describe how my mother often told me, "David, honey, you are so smart you could be anything you want to be. Really, honey."

When I told this story to kids, I could see they really liked it. So I started saying it to the entire audience. Then I realized the power of such an encounter, and I began approaching three or four students, looking each one in the eye from a couple of feet away and telling them, "You are so smart, you could be anything you want to be. Really, honey." And their faces lit up.

A month or so after we did a *Love at Second Sight* live presentation at which I had said that to several kids, I received an email from a girl who wrote: "When you looked me in the eye and told me I was beautiful and smart, I believed that I was beautiful and smart. And now I know I am." This thrilled me beyond measure and encouraged me to say those words to students more often, knowing that they could be life-changing for them.

Interestingly, though, I had not told that girl that she was beautiful. I only told her she was smart. She had understood the beautiful part as a bonus. I think any child who is told eye to eye that they are smart—or anything positive and from the heart—can carry that in their heart for life.

That was a moment of grace that will live on for me and for all those who hear it.

Listen to Your Own Story: Storytelling and the Emergence of the New Self

S torytelling is one of the primal human arts, along with music, dance and cave drawing. Stories beguile, inform and entertain, serving to knit families together, build community and inculcate religious and cultural values.

When individuals tell their own stories, the process can be deeply transformative. Storytelling fills a fundamental human need to share who we are and what we have learned, to imagine and dream. And when you listen to your own story, it can change your life.

Dana is getting ready for storytelling night. Whenever I encountered her in the week before, she announced she was nervous. She knew the story she wanted to tell but proclaimed, "I am just not a storyteller."

Now, on story night, as Dana steps through the front door, she again proclaims her anxiety. It turns out she has written down her story.

In my experience as a storytelling coach, pre-writing a story is common. People tend to prepare a story in advance in the belief that this will present a semblance of competence and hide their self-perceived flaws. Their frontal lobes try to stay in control, wanting desperately to present a story that is coherent and makes sense. The fear can be intense and feel insurmountable. There is a consolation to be obtained, however: that fear is commonly disproportionate to the reality of the storytelling experience. Once one is able to look out to and feel the supportive energy of the listeners, the fear often instantaneously deflates. It matters not whether the story is written out and read or is spoken in an ad-lib style.

Dana's characteristic determination has brought her here. She steps in front of the group to read aloud her story of being five years old and in a conflict with her younger brother about marbles she has been playing with. Her brother pockets one of the marbles; they struggle over it while her mother calls out (unsuccessfully) from the next room to get them to stop. At one point, Dana is on top of her brother trying to strangle him. She is fully present in the story moment as she describes the pressure she's exerting on his hyoid bone. The story is resolved when Dana brings her adult self back to the present moment to imagine apologizing to her brother.

It is a brilliant story on a universal theme and very well told, with many of the elements I strive to emphasize in my own storytelling: good dialogue smoothly delivered, well cadenced and articulated. Most important is her use of sensory detail. Those kinds of concrete details (the marbles, being on top of her brother) serve as a portal for the listener to step into the story with Dana. She gets great feedback, and part of the reason is that she has avoided the use of abstraction.

Abstract concepts are empty vessels that the presenter or the listener each have to fill in their own way—their meanings might be entirely different. Abstractions are like acronyms. They only have meaning when delivered to an audience that has predetermined their meaning.

One of Dana's universal themes is that of the forgiveness asked of her brother and the forgiveness given implicitly to herself. This is one of the characteristics of deep soul stories. In the world of transformational storytelling, there is no time lapse from Dana's five-year-old life to the present day. If the soul asks you to tell a certain story, it can immediately come to life in the present.

I am struck by what Dana has done because I had believed the nervousness declarations. In fact, she displayed no anxiety at all. This is another common phenomenon; a huge disparity can exist between the storyteller's self-judgment and what the listeners perceive.

Three weeks later Dana speaks at Hazel Bell-Koski's art show launch at the Gumboot Café. I am the MC and have arranged to have Dana signal from the audience whether she is willing to talk about the lovely prayer flags on which she and Hazel have collaborated. She nods her assent from the audience, and comes to the mic. She is a strong presence and delivers. That night, and then again two nights later, she asks me how she did.

"You know, the words you said were fine, the delivery was fine, you brought it right to the audience, you had their full attention and you segued well to the part where you intro'd Hazel. The main thing is that you radiated presence and power. That's the core of what you have. You have a gift; your presence is 80 percent of what you have to offer. The words were of secondary importance."

Dana does indeed have the type of presence that changes people as soon as she walks into a room. That's the kind of story she truly lives. The key to presence is not the mastery of technique, it is being fully yourself.

"Being fully yourself" sounds like the slogan of a new-age social media guru. How do you know you are fully yourself when standing in front of a group telling a story?

Start by being present in the room. Don't begin telling your story until you look around the room, look at your audience, see the warmth in their eyes. Take a couple of deep breaths and smile at them. Take a slight bow toward them, a slight inclination of your head.

Separate yourself from the story. One way to do this is to listen to yourself as you tell the story. Know also that you are not telling a story, you are relating to the listeners. The story has come alive in your imagination, and it arcs into the hearts and minds of the listeners, where it truly comes alive. It is not about you, it's about relationship and the community that is being built. The story does not belong to you; it is a gift you have brought to others. Your story is being born in community and nurtured there; the listeners are part of your presence—they love it and want more.

Just like many other people, when Dana confronts the possibility of finding her own strong voice and demonstrating how she has done just that, her brain still lives in the old story: "I am nervous, I won't remember, I don't know what to say, I fear embarrassment."

My observation, based on thirty years of experience as a speaker and performer with a facial difference is that, as social animals, we all carry the generic and encultured fear that we are inherently simply unacceptable and unlovable. Belief in original sin or bad karma are examples of contributing factors to that belief.

So Dana does not yet recognize her own new story as it is being born, even as new Dana is popping out into the world. The old story still has a grip on her.

We all tend to live in our old stories. Sometimes this means old stories from a religion, a culture, a family, that have been laid on us since birth. I spent many years of my adult life being a good Catholic boy trying to do the right thing. (Actually, that is still true.) In the meantime, alcohol blunted my soul's desires and my creativity.

I did not begin to find my own story until I got on stage in my mid-forties. First I had to quit alcohol, and then I found my soulmate. Love and sobriety led to finding and voicing my own creativity. Even then, it took years to be comfortable as myself. That involved telling my story hundreds of times to thousands of people and listening to them tell me how wonderful I was and how I changed their lives. For a long time, I thought they were just being polite to a disfigured guy.

I did a long, slow story change, as do many people. This makes me sensitive to a similar process in others, and now I see that happening with Dana. She gets in front of an audience and the new Dana is emerging while in her mind she still lives back with the old Dana.

It is so easy to get stuck in our forebrains, our consciousness, as we try to get control over our lives. We look to the writings of others—books, podcasts, workshops—most all of which are marketed to us. We tune in to data transmitted into our brains while tending to ignore our own wisdom, our own hearts and souls. We don't even know we have our own story, let alone listen to it.

This is why it is important to listen to your own story. Don't let your consciousness try to force a correct story on you. Instead, listen to what is coming from inside. It doesn't have to be planned. Sometimes it just springs up; you think you are telling one story, then suddenly it changes.

Oftentimes our voices are stilled. "Children should be seen and not heard." I am ignorant, I am not the expert. Women, people of colour, the disabled—people are voiceless for any number of reasons. Sometimes, too, we silence ourselves, and one way that can happen is when we do not listen to our own voices. When we pause, we try to fill up the empty space with any kind of chatter instead of taking the time to listen to our own souls. The pause is a place where we can and should listen to ourselves. This can often be a key time, the starting point for listening to our own new story.

That starting point can also come "off-story"—outside of the story. It is important to honour pauses in storytelling, and the same is true in daily life. Pauses can come in the form of meditation or reflection, tuning in to quiet space where you may find rich story material—for example, in the remembrance of things past or in the emergence of raw, unexpected feelings. All good story stuff. Keep your ears open to listen to your heart and your gut.

There is nothing inherently wrong with old stories, by the way. For example, that is one of the ways that families are held together, that cultures are built and nurtured. A key factor in keeping my marriage strong is that I listen every morning to the story about how Marlena slept the night before.

I can't wait to hear Dana's next story.

My Chihuahua, Frank

I walk into a Grade 6 classroom. The kids have met me before, and this time the principal has told me they've had incidents of teasing and some bullying. She wants me to visit them. I don't know exactly what to do, so I impulsively announce the launch of the David Roche Beauty School. (After all, who needs it more than twelve-year-olds?)

"Kids, I want to hear who in your life is really beautiful."

Laurie, with black hair and black-rimmed glasses, has her hand up before I finish my sentence. "Frank is beautiful. My chihuahua, Frank."

I am a little surprised, but the other students are not. Three others raise their hands when they hear this.

"My pit bull!"

I'm sure I look astonished. "So, okay, tell us how your pit bull is beautiful."

"Well ... well, when I lie down on the couch, he comes and lies down behind me ..." She gestures to her back and students nearby nod in understanding. "And he pretends to, like, stretch, you know, but really, he's pushing me off the couch. And that is beautiful."

I laugh with the students. "Yes, that is beautiful."

In the front row, Trevor, with a vibrantly warm personality and fetal alcohol syndrome, raises his hand. "My bunny, Honey Bunny. He's so beautiful."

Will he get teased for this? No. More hands in the air. They are completely rapt and into the exercise.

Megan has a round face framed with strawberry-blond hair. "My grandma. She had two strokes but still cooks dinner for us. Every night. And she won't sit down until we start eating. I think that is beautiful. She is beautiful."

"Oh, a beautiful *person*. Thank you. Good. She sounds very kind. I think kindness is a sign of beauty, don't you?"

They all nod yes. Vigorously.

"Well, who do we know in this room who is kind? Let's have some kindness beauty nominations."

"Nancy is kind."

"Who is Nancy? Is she here today?"

Half of the class points at Nancy, who responds by drawing in her shoulders, staring down at her desk and flushing.

"How is Nancy kind?"

"She always says hi in the hall every morning."

"Friendliness," I say. "That is a sign of kindness."

The girls continue to lead the way.

"Briana. When I don't feel good, she asks me if I'm okay."

"Kate. She took me to the nurse when I got hit in the face with a basketball and stayed through lunch."

I intercede. "Now I want to get the guys involved. I want to hear nominations for boys with beautiful kindness." Turns out they just had to be asked.

"Sean is kind."

"How?"

"Umm, he shares his dirt bike. And his Wii."

"Wow, sharing your dirt bike! That is special. That's beautiful kindness."

"Gord, because when I'm playing soccer and make a mistake, he tells me it's okay, and then I know it is."

I am astounded at the depth of what I'm hearing.

The acknowledged boys tend to be more impassive. Perhaps I should not have used the word beauty. But they certainly get the kindness part.

"Danny always helps us in art class. He shows us what to do so it's easier."

Danny's head pops up. He is a little guy with a punk hairdo, carrying an air of toughness and bravado. He is startled; he's been outed as an art angel.

"Two good examples. Someone who encourages you when you're down, like when you made a mistake. Especially in sports, right, guys?"

The boys nod. A couple have small, wry grins.

"I wish I'd had someone like you when I was your age, Danny."

Megan's hand is up again; she's looking at me expectantly. I call on her.

"Well, I have acne and some people think that's weird or gross, but my friends don't worry about that."

Her straightforwardness, her calm tone of voice belies her age. This is a twelve-year-old?

"Who are they?"

"Sofia. Claire."

"Sofia, is that true?"

Sofia lights up. "Yes."

I see Tom, in the front row, hesitating. "Go ahead."

"Well ... well, I can be pretty wild and some people think that's strange, but when I came here I didn't act wild until I met Patrick, and he's kind of wild too, so we got to be friends and now I act wild and I like it."

The time is winding down. "Thank you all so much," I say.

Laurie is waving her hand.

"Okay, Laurie, one more."

Laurie takes control of the class: "Who hasn't been nominated yet?"

They all look around and point at the ones who haven't had their kindness acknowledged. They start in again without my participation and go past the bell (the *lunch* bell!). They want to finish the job. They do. Everyone gets a kindness nomination. Everyone. Even the teacher. They are sincere and thoughtful nominations.

The teacher says: "Okay, class over." They all rush out.

On the drive home, I miss the students fiercely. That was so much fun. I am proud and excited about the launch of the David Roche Beauty School. I start wondering. How can you tell that someone is beautiful? I like this question. Maybe it should be: What are the ten signs of beauty? Is kindness really one of those signs (or was I just pushing that on the kids)?

Well, I thought, kindness would get my vote. Maybe that could be an introductory course in the David Roche Beauty School. We could address important questions like: How do you encourage someone when they make a mistake in sports? How do you tell when someone needs encouragement? Is it difficult to be kind? Where did you learn to be kind?

I wish I had pointed out to the kids that all their examples were of inner beauty (except maybe for Honey Bunny and Frank the chihuahua), that we all want to look good, but what people truly care about is how we act. Then I realize that they were the ones with examples and I was the one who was surprised.

That's enough. I slip out of self-improvement mode, sigh, relax into the beauty of the day and exult in the moments of grace the kids have given me.

The Kingdom of Heaven

I walk into the RayCam Co-operative Centre on the Downtown Eastside of Vancouver (DTES). I'm about to lead a storytelling workshop. I do not know who will be there.

The hallways are filled with kids bouncing about, filled with just-got-out-of-school energy. My escort appears, and I find out we are headed to the girls' club.

There are a couple of dozen girls, ages eight to eleven, who are girling about, chatting and hugging. They are DTES-diverse, as are the women who work with them. Kaia is in charge. I am the only man among thirty women and girls. They do not pay much attention to me.

Mila, one of the tiniest, comes and stands in front of me. "What happened to your face?" She is curious and friendly, not at all wary or judging.

"Thank you for asking. I'll tell you in just a few minutes." She nods and skips back to her chair.

At Kaia's direction, they begin to settle down and form a

circle, all sitting in little kindergarten-sized chairs. I introduce myself as a performer. "I'm shy. I need your help. When I count one, two, three, I need you to ask all together: 'What happened to your face?'"

And so they do, in unison.

"I was born this way. My veins got too big and they kind of went wild." I tell about being loved in my family. I stand up, go to several girls one by one, look them in the eye just as I'd described my mother doing for me, and I say, with a slower tempo and in a notch-lower register: "Honey, you are so smart. You could be anything you want to be. Anything. Really, honey." I repeat that to several more of them. With each girl I approach, my heart opens more and I see in their eyes that they believe me.

Then comes my story of Nana telling me to hold my chin up. When I become Nana yelling at me to be proud of myself, I am loud. Little Sarah clutches Kaia. "Oh, was I too loud?" I ask, and Kaia gives me a nod of reassurance.

"Now," I say, a little more softly, "those women on TV, they just look weird with that strange makeup. They don't look like real people. I don't think they are beautiful. I want to know who in your life is naturally beautiful and what makes them that way."

First is Keisha, a little older than the others. In response to being urged to join the circle, she has placed herself facing half in, half out. "I haven't seen my sister in a while." Her voice trails off. She wipes her eyes. Conscious only of her, I cross the room, fishing in my pocket for a clean tissue.

"Your sister … what is beautiful about her?"

"She loves me, she cares for me. I don't know where she is." I wait. She retreats into her silent grief. I go back to my chair.

Meena says, waving her hand, "He wants us to feel good about ourselves the way we are," and others nod.

Keisha turns her chair into the circle. She doesn't raise her hand, she just starts speaking again. Her tone, her cadence are different. She points out her cousin Lexi and Lexi's sister Marianne across the room and tells how wonderful and beautiful they are. They hide their faces, giggle and squirm. Lexi dips out of sight behind Marianne's chair.

Keisha, not me, sets the tone, first by her vulnerability, then with her leadership of the younger girls, and in both cases, it is about family. We are witnessing healing.

Serena can't weigh more than forty pounds. She has clear reasons why Katie is beautiful. "She's always friendly. She doesn't tease, ever." Katie's eyes glow. Her face lights up; she soaks in the acknowledgement. "And she looks like Katy Perry." This brings general laughter.

They love this exercise; they easily see, call out and cling to beauty in others. The mood blossoms. Shyer girls begin to speak.

Serena stands and crosses the circle. She stands in front of caregiver Sonia, face to face, and tells her, "You are beautiful because you take care of so many kids and you don't forget anyone. You look good in that black-and-white striped top." After a beat, she says, "The shoes look good too."

They call out signs of beauty in others: She is kind. She takes care of me. She is nice to me when I'm sad. She likes to play with me. She walks me to school every day. I like it when I go to her house. She is cuddly. She likes to hug. She signs for her mother. Her hair is messy and she doesn't care, she still is beautiful.

Often, they jump up and race across to one another with enthusiastic hugs. Pop-up love. The circle begins to draw inward as they reach to one another.

I hold up my hand and announce that *kind* and *nice* are the words they are using to identify beauty. Even as I speak, I recede into the background. They are feasting on each other's friendship. The girls who are being outed as beautiful bask in what the others say.

Kaia starts to take charge, making sure all the girls get heard. Kaia has a delicate, loving touch. She knows how to bring out the quiet ones, the shy ones, those new to the group; they respond to her encouragement.

Lexi wants to speak. I do not know this is the case, even when I am looking right at her. I cannot hear her, even from six feet away. It sounds as if she is inhaling her words. Her friends understand, however. I ask one of them for help, and she repeats Lexi's words after her. The other girls give her total attention. Lexi is not really shy; she has just been waiting for the perfect words. She talks about how love is important, and I see that Keisha's earlier encouragement has led Lexi to also take a leadership position.

I am witnessing miracles.

This runs on for almost an hour. Once in a while I say something, but by the end I have nothing much to do with the flow of the group. By then they are clamouring to identify as beautiful two, three, half a dozen other girls at a time. It's a recognition of how beauty is relational, a community thing.

At the end they all agree (more or less) to tell someone new that they are beautiful. Kaia tells them to "clap it in," and we all clap: *one, two, three.* Kaia says, "Let's dance," and we all jump up for a minute's worth of joyful movement. Then, "Group hug!" I join in (a little tentatively) and we all hold one another, and the whole group turns in a circle.

In a few seconds they chatter and scatter, off to other activities, many of them with their arms around each other.

On Set

The gear of a movie set is crowded into the foyer of a fourth-floor apartment on Queen Mary Boulevard in Montreal. Crew members stand silently around me. From one of the bedrooms, where she and Alexandre and Florence are watching the monitor, assistant director Alexandra calls "first positions," and I stand ready.

A year and a half ago, in 2016, director/*réalisateur* Alexandre Franchi contacted me about a role in *Happy Face*, a film set in a support group for people with facial differences. I read the script and was shocked, dubious and yet intrigued by his artistic vision and willingness to go to the edge. I auditioned via Skype and was offered a principal role. I accepted because Alexandre planned to cast a number of amateurs who had facial disfigurements. I saw it as a social responsibility to my community and a chance to raise the profile of those with facial differences.

As the time to leave for Montreal approached, I grew resentful and self-pitying. "People will make fun of me. I'm too old to do this kind of shit. I'm being taken advantage of. Francophones will be rude because I only speak *un peu* French. Disability activists will accuse me of being politically incorrect." And so on.

Now, when I appear at a September 30 rehearsal, everything changes. There is an instant sense of camaraderie, of *famille.* Everyone is personable, kind, encouraging and funny.

At the first shoot, Debbie, in the role of support-group facilitator Vanessa, begins with, "Let me tell you a little bit about myself." Her ability to step into character enchants me. During seven takes for the scene I watch her go deeper and deeper into the role of Vanessa. I think, *Oh my God, is this how it's done? I could never do that as well as she does.* But still, I feel I can do it. I feel an upwelling of confidence. This is the first of many acting lessons.

All through October, I stay in a B&B in the Le Village area of Montreal. Out the window, a sea of trees daily changes colour and decorates sidewalks. Drizzly days are especially *charmant.* I succumb to this 375-year-old city (especially the boulangeries) and its beauty. Mostly people live in apartments that are very well built, though they are aging (the apartments, I mean), as is the rest of the city. The neighbourhood has no yards; people are out on the street. Except I don't see many people in wheelchairs on the crumbling sidewalks.

I am one of the early arrivals (6:45 a.m.) on the fourth day of shooting on location at Royal Victoria Hospital, which had been abandoned for years. Robin and I are the only early actors; our footsteps click time as we head down empty hallways, past decrepit laboratories to the makeshift/pop-up dressing room on the second floor. Robin observes that it feels as though we are on the set of a horror film.

Wardrobe, makeup, hair styling, the crew, all are scurrying and bustling to get set up. Full intensity starts immediately and will not end for twelve hours. Robin pitches in to help move tables and chairs. I follow his lead. As more actors arrive, they are scooped up by wardrobe and scrupulous attention to detail begins. Mohamed and Guy have been up late washing clothes and preparing the outfits each person will wear; their workdays are much longer than mine.

My character is Otis. He is the same age as I am (seventy-three) and wears well-made wool gabardine pants, cuffed, pleated, lined, with ample drape all the way around and down. Today, a dark-striped cotton shirt, also well made, over a white cotton tee. Sheepskin jacket. Bruno Magli loafers. Everything fits well and is appropriate for Otis in 1991, if not for David Roche in 2017. But I appreciate the quality of the clothes and wonder whether I should go fashion retro in real life.

On the second day of shooting, I wear a turquoise-y heavy cardigan, the kind we used to call a Perry Como sweater. (You can Google Perry Como, so I won't explain further.) I first try it on during September rehearsals, and I do not like how it looks. Not at all. I show a photo to Marlena, who agrees with me. I take the trouble to write to Myléne, the production manager and production co-ordinator. She is fiercely busy, but kind enough to relay my hatred of the sweater to Alexandre, who in turn reassures me that he would veto it but also hold it in reserve in case I did not bring my inner madness to the Otis role.

But Guy and Mohamed do not get the message and lay out the sweater for me. I complain immediately to Mohamed, who earnestly reassures me that I look great. "Anyway, you are no longer David. You are now Otis." Which gives me pause. *What does it matter what David thinks? It's Otis who's wearing it.* I get a compliment from Valerie about how it brings out my beautiful eyes. Which gives me more pause. Several other compliments come my way, and I went from whine to preen.

No makeup is needed for Otis. He comes in makeup free. Or rather, wearing makeup by God. Otis's hair takes about twenty-three seconds. Combing down the cut-short sides, a little fluff of what is left up top, a swish of spray and done. As I leave, Mohamed stops me to do a once-over and adjusts my collar.

Stephane drives me to the day's first scene in front of the Royal Vic, where '90s cars are parked to establish authenticity. It's a simple scene, but nothing is done without incredible care.

A conference is taking place as I arrive. Director of photography Claudine is always (to me) amazingly joyful. I love to watch her survey the ambience of the shoot-to-be. The sky, the windows of the hospital, the cars, the colour of the sidewalk that Robin and I are about to traverse. She takes it all in, and she and her assistant Thierry make camera adjustments. Nothing is taken for granted.

Here is the sequence: Robin and I on our marks (chalked on the sidewalk). The scene is called out and the scene marker held in front of the camera. Thierry calls out "marker," and it is clicked. After a few beats Claudine calls *motor* (i.e., the camera is rolling). Then *action*, and off we go until *coupé* ends the scene.

The other main scene drivers are assistant director Alexandra and director Alexandre Franchi. And always hovering nearby is Florence, the one most responsible for continuity. For example, on the fourth take of a scene later that day, she reminds me that on the first take I started the scene holding my head in my palm and then lifting it as I began my lines.

In this scene I accompany the character played by Robin into the hospital on a fraught personal journey. Robin is an incredibly talented actor; as we walk side by side, I absorb his feelings and it almost overwhelms me. This has an amazing buoying effect, which I feel often during the shoot. As Robin tells me, it's a group effort.

I love this experience: the director, the crew, my fellow actors. I am learning so much. It will be a great movie. It has sex (not for Otis, however), a little violence, dancing, humour.

Back to the apartment on Queen Mary. I am wearing black leather pants, a red-trimmed black Michael Jackson jacket and bright-red plastic shoes. I have just been in a scene shot outside in driving rain that, in the final film, will directly precede the scene we are shooting now. My hair is perforce still wet; rivulets run down my face. I am holding a dripping wet black Borsalino fedora. I hear Alexandre's *action*, step forward and see Robin through the open door of the *toilette* to my left. Unaware of my entrance into his apartment, he is loading toilet articles into a plastic bag. I take it all in for a nanosecond, discard the hat on a nearby coat rack, approach the doorway of the *toilette* and stand there.

Claudine and Thierry have slipped behind me with the camera. I have already lost any immediate sense of their presence.

Robin, less than three feet away, stares into the middle distance of the mirror over the sink. I wait silently, watching. He slips out of his reverie, sees me in the mirror and says, "Go away."

I move a step closer, driven by a cellular desire to enter into the story that he is living. "I am not leaving. Not this time."

Our spoken words are real and meaningful but also serve as portals to a deeper flow that beckons us. "Come. I will take you to her."

I am offering Robin's character the gift of support in dealing with his mother's impending death. Our relationship, only a few days old, has been marked with emotional contention and threatened physical violence. I have finally begun to see his fuller humanity and to offer him what an elder can offer a young man.

I am wrapped in the force that, in his fear and grief, he is radiating. I cannot name it, but it is irresistible. I feel a swelling in my throat, in my heart.

The tone, cadence, volume, register and timbre of our voices blend. Those qualities, not our words, are what most reveals both our backstories and our yearning for healing. Past and future have folded into this present moment, not compressed but flowing together in a deep channel. In this moment we are freed from the chains of human consciousness, so fraught with remembered resentments and fear-laden tomorrows. We are in the flow of love.

I am the elder here, he is the youth. He is facing something new and terrible, and I can help him.

The crew is silent, far in the background of my awareness. The notes that Alexandre gave me are coming alive, partially through my agency but mostly by the atmosphere Robin creates.

I remember to step back to where Claudine had directed me, to the right, against the doorway, but not leaning. She needs a good angle to capture Robin.

"I want her to die."

"Robin, when someone we love is dying, we want them to

leave so we do not feel the pain of their suffering. Everybody feels that way. It is okay, it is natural."

With one simple sentence, Robin speaks with the voices of billions who have feared facing the death of a loved one. "I don't know what to do."

My voice slows and slips into a lower register. "I will drive you. I will wait for you. I will drive you home. I will bring you food. I will help you to get through this."

The scene is over, but far in the back of my brain I hear Alexandre: "Keep rolling." I feel a spurt of exultation, then step back into the hum of creation. Robin is the creator here and I follow him, but in this moment, there is no distinction between us. He steps into an eternal silent minute and then begins to weep.

"When you walk into her room, all of life's shittiness will still be there. But all you have to do is two things. Hold her hand. Breathe. Repeat. Repeat. As you do, all of that shittiness, the craziness, stupidity, fear, her scars and yours, they all begin to fade away. The only thing left before you will be love. Let it in as much as you can. Open your heart and that love will last you the rest of your life."

The camera holds and soaks up Robin's face. Then, "*Coupé.*"

I bounce into the room where Alexandre, Alexandra and Florence have been watching the monitor. I look at them, I know I am a part of them and the rest of the crew, and I feel the power of the group collaboration that created this scene.

It isn't just Robin and me. We are held by so many others. And not only those present on set. In the scene, I was back in the AIDS epidemic in San Francisco and I remembered how my friends had died, and all those stored memories surfaced and spoke through me. My cells remembered David Kleinberg dying of AIDS, stripped of any sense of time, flesh wasted, just a soul lying there thirsting, ready to roll off of life into the river of love. We wiped off his waste and all that was left was soul. Fungi, bacteria, viruses, all eager to do their duty, stripped him down to soul alone. What a sight and what a smell and what a sound of coughing out what was no longer needed by the soul. How could it be so beautiful when it smelled so bad?

In the scene, I spoke not from Montreal but from Pacific Presbyterian Hospital, where Marlena and I gave massages to patients as they moved toward death. I cried out from Jim Steinemann's room, my hands on him as he died in misery with a giant, swollen, bright-yellow body.

In that scene with Robin, time collapsed. Images and emotions appeared but not details. Everything melted away until there was just me and Robin—but the whole world moved with us and within us.

Love You to Death
and How that Works

It's November 2017. I am with Syd Valentine in room 204 of Sechelt Hospital. I have brought her the nonalcoholic beer and Clamato she craves. She guzzles down a huge glassful as she gazes out at the cedars and the diamonds of sun on the Salish Sea.

"This is called a Redeye. Always been my favourite. It's the only thing I can keep down now."

Six feet tall, sixty years old, slim and stately in her hospital gown, with short grey hair and a warm, expressive face, Syd is lovely, filled with light, filled with cancer and nearing death.

"I signed the MAID papers and I feel happier than I ever have in my whole life. I have no more responsibilities. The only thing I regret is not taking more time off. That's it."

I stare at her, I take her in. She is at ease. I look into eyes alight with warmth. The eyes of a dying woman? They crinkle with laughter. My eyes, my brain, do not understand. I begin to listen with the rest of me, but I am not used to this way of learning.

I know Syd only because I patronized her video store, but I followed the lead of Laurie Verchomin and came to visit.

December 2017
Around Syd in her hospital room are Laurie O'Byrne, Laurie Verchomin, Gerry Hills and me. This is our writing group. We talk, we write. Now, in this room, a vortex of female energy and leadership and trust is forming. But it's not yet time for her to die.

My fondest desire is to be articulate, funny, charming. That is what I do. That is who I am. That is my sell. But that's a no go here. In this situation, I find I speak from outside myself as I search for safety, for sustenance of some sort, for *je ne sais quoi* in the face of impending death. It's not just diminution of social skills, of coping mechanisms. There is a deeper tremble present in me.

These women, they are more present than me. They surround, see Syd in the moment, they see her past life and how it brought her to this time, to her hospital bed, they see and hear how she built that life, all her woman's choices, and they honour her. I feel apart from them yet fully with them—I am learning, I am holding onto things I thought I knew even though I did not know what I thought I knew. I feel there must be something here for me to hold onto, maybe some temporary belief just to get by, just to understand what is going on.

January 2018
CAT scan results tell Syd the time has come. The writing group is gathering this afternoon at the hospital, but it will not be about writing. It will be about planning death. I've decided not to go because I am embarrassed. In truth, I feel ashamed and

unworthy. I see myself as shallow, self-centred, feigning love. It's a January-dark-day moment for me. I fear, I ache, I withhold. The women proceed without me. But before a half hour passes, I have a change of heart. Even though I'm not with them, I feel this group of women's love for Syd so strongly that I push my misgivings aside and join them.

Much texting takes place as death day is organized. "Yes," they tell Syd, "it will be at Laurie and Brock's home." "Yes, you will die in a beautiful place; you can see the forest and the sea from there. There will be room for those who love you to death."

Syd will do invites. Does her son Yosichi approve? Is January 28 a good day? Syd texts and confirms the physicians. Death is scheduled, and Syd wants music, joy, laughter. The love that will surround death has already manifested.

Penny Allport and Marlena are with us now. Penny suggests we all write Syd's obituary. Her life story flows into the room and our hearts. Leaving Nova Scotia for the University of British Columbia at age sixteen. Wild and free, resilient and self-defining. A shooting star tells her she is pregnant with Yosichi. Single motherhood. Swinging a toolbelt for Telus. Finding her place in Roberts Creek, working at the Gumboot Café and then starting Syd's Vids, in so many ways in the heart of the Sunshine Coast, a place where customers became friends and community was built while Yosichi grew into manhood.

Yosichi, twenty-four, is in the Canadian Forces, stationed in Alberta. He has been given all the leave he needs to be with his mother at this time. As a medic, he can and does give her injections, and she remarks on how this is a bond for them. She wishes she could be with her son to see how he grows. This is the first time I have seen the mask of sadness fall over her face, but it is of the moment, sadness acknowledged and fully felt but not clung to.

Syd says she realized she'd been trying to push herself into the future, but it did not work. She saw she had to stay in the moment, in the last moments of life. Now she fills those moments connecting with her visitors.

January 28, 5:00 a.m.
Up early with random, tumbling thoughts and freestyle feelings. Today Syd will die at 4:00 p.m.

I go to church with Marlena, the first time in decades I have gone without a funeral or a wedding as the reason. I don't know why, don't know what I want outside of some sense of ease. There is comfort to be obtained from the music, though I find myself wishing for older, more familiar hymns.

This day will unfold without a plan. There is no way of knowing what it will hold except for death and a party before the death.

Syd does not want any kind of ceremony. Penny sees this; she is a seasoned death watcher, a keen observer of the dying process. We all are following Syd's wishes, and that means waiting, watching, following the flow of the day, the unfolding of a life ticking toward death.

I remember my mother's funeral, one of the worst experiences of my life. In a Catholic church, a priest spoke of her as she lay in the coffin, and there was no sense of her heart and soul, what her life meant, her legacy. I sat in the front pew in stunned rage.

Today there will be a party, a gathering from 1:00 to 4:00 p.m., and then the doctors come, and then, then what? Syd dies? Is that what will happen? I think Marlena knows what will happen. No, no, she doesn't, but she is not concerned that she does not know. She is fine with just being present. I hope I am. I want an emotional swag bag to take home with me.

All the constructs from my past are missing. No memes. Only ones that will be born this afternoon.

There come washes of love through me, some primal yearning caressing me. This is how life should be always, this is the way that it could be if women had charge.

Be it resolved: Be present with her, be present for her. No rituals, only a life well lived brought forward into Brock and Laurie's house. A blessing for their house, for all of us. A strange and unknown blessing. I hope I am open to it.

January 28, 1:00 p.m.
It is, it is! We wanted the day to be what Syd wants it to be, and that is what happens. Marlena and I are greeters. Some forty warm and fully feeling faces appear at the door. Two twelve-year-olds walk in bearing red licorice vines to tell Syd thank you for having had her video store.

Syd, in flowing white lace, lies back on the couch, friends gathering around for greetings, hugs, tears, giving and receiving love. She reaches out her hand to all, remains radiant, lit from within with beauty. Her legacy, a living legacy, surrounds her; she is a leader unto death, claiming ownership of her death as she did her life.

I had been so afraid of this day, had arrived with a brain filled with Catholic childhood memories that told me what should happen. Then the *shoulds* melt around the edges and are washed away by the love in this house.

People gather in a weaving together with those they know and those they do not know. This is a day for the touchers to gently rub a back, an arm, a shoulder. We lean into one another's humanity, so easy to find today. This is not a day about death, this is a day about community. Syd has led us here.

As at any kind of family or social gathering, people congregate at the food table for emotional sustenance. There I find Billy Hume and Aaron Joe, both warm-hearted men, and I want to be near them. As we stand there, I can picture myself with Billy at his stand at the farmers' market and with Aaron at Salish Soils. Any individual connections at Syd's event radiate out. I feel in place at this occasion, in Roberts Creek, on the Sunshine Coast, in this community of heart, and in the world.

Brad and Derek and Justin, young men who congregated at the video store for years to play games, are the ones among us who look most distraught. They had been at the store more consistently, gotten to know Syd better than the rest of us, worked closely with her; they were there for her diagnosis and for the closing of a Sunshine Coast institution.

I step to the back door, to the deck that looks out on the Salish Sea, to a pondering place, to gather my wits and take in the dreary grey day. I turn and see the house glowing into the rainforest around us.

I see, I see. I slip into, out of and around different realities. A crack in time, a crack in the day, a crack in my consciousness, they all align. Suddenly my eyes track to my heart, not my brain, and beauty is more easily seen in the day, in the sky and the sea. Beauty too in the concrete deck, in the cedar flakes that abound there, in the ashtray where the smokers gather that somehow seems a portal to the beauty of the universe felt for a nanosecond.

This is at its core a woman's day, a day created by Syd over the course of her lifetime, a day when we see her life come to fruition. Over the last couple of months she came to see and state what she wanted, and what she wanted was what she had lived and created. And today it is flowing all around her, holding her.

I ask people how they came to know Syd. For many, it was through the store. They entered as customers, left as friends. Amazing people are here today. Sally is sitting by herself. I go and sit by her. She had been a secretary at Ontario's largest psychiatric hospital for twenty-five years. She says she has always been a people watcher. She sits and watches people's auras. "All kinds today."

January 28, 3:45 p.m.
Syd is scheduled to start the dying process in about fifteen minutes. We have music. Dave Morgan plays "Amazing Grace" on a banjo that Syd has given him. That familiar tune picked out on an instrument that usually does not voice it. The simplicity, the slowed-down timing, call us together.

I want to find people to sing "Amazing Grace" with me. Laurie O'Byrne says yes immediately. There is no time for rehearsal. It is not about the notes. I don't worry about being on key; I just bring it as best I can. Laurie Verchomin joins us, Boyd Norman steps in. The room is singing with us. I am not looking at Syd. I am in and of the gathering.

> *Through many dangers, toils and snares*
> *I have already come.*
> *'Twas grace that brought me safe thus far*
> *And grace shall lead me home.*

Boyd does a solo, a lullaby about a baby falling asleep and waking to a new day.

People weep silently.

While we sing, Syd leaves the couch and stands at the top of the steps, halfway to the place set out for her to die. "More music!" she says, so Laurie sings a Van Morrison song.

Syd reaches out for final hugs.

There is no narrative, no chronology. What is linear dissolves.

I had been around death but had never been around a deliberately chosen death. But no, it was not deliberately chosen. Death made the choice, cancer made the choice and Syd negotiated the terms.

In the moments as she steps down to the lovely daybed, all tapestried, where she is going to die, Syd continues to teach us about the good death, to lead us toward our own dying. She lies down surrounded by flowers and friends.

> *Swing low, sweet chariot*
> *Coming for to carry me home*
> *Roberts Creek is chilly and cold*
> *Coming for to carry me home*
> *Chills the body but not the soul*
> *Coming for to carry me home*
> *Looked over to the island and what did I see*
> *Coming for to carry me home*
> *A canoe full of friends coming for me*
> *Coming for to carry me home*
> *Swing low, sweet friends of mine*
> *Coming for to carry me home*
> *The creek flows into the ocean now*
> *Coming for to carry me home.*

The doctors arrive. They said in advance that Syd should have privacy as she dies, but as they enter the house they change their minds. They see us singing, dancing. Syd wants to die in our presence; Yosichi agrees. We find our places, some nearby, some farther away.

I look down on her from near the top of the stairs. She is calm. She holds Yosichi's hand. He is calm. He smiles at her. The injections start, the first one a sedative, and she relaxes. Then five more, one by one. Syd does not move, but her facial muscles relax. Her beauty remains. As the minutes go by, her jaw drops slightly, her face pales.

Some people silently cry. Most just watch sombrely.

Oh, dear God, this is not a day of death. It is a day of acceptance, of giving, of the easing of fear, of community. Love has conquered death. I have seen it. I have felt it. Love conquers death.

I want to take it all in so it will last the rest of my life. My brain runs around barking wildly. The rest of me reaches without effort or choice to the love about me, the beauty of human beings in the thrum of the universe.

I had wanted to identify and categorize my feelings, to understand them. Now, all the self-searching of the last few months seems so futile and foolish. As I stand next to Syd, I am nothing but present, alone yet fully with Syd and with everyone in the room. It is far beyond anything physical, nothing but pure presence, a feeling beyond feeling. I do not know what that presence is, but it doesn't matter.

January 30, 2018, 5:00 a.m.
I wake early again, still present in the events of two days ago. In the dark Canadian winter night, this is what came to me:

As she died, Syd gave us life and the love of life. That is how I see the beauty, that is how I lose my fear. Oh my God, she died for us. That's what Jesus did. And Syd rises again this morning in my mind, in my heart, in my memory, in my imagination. I have never known what gratitude is—until now.

Being Listened To

Kathleen asked whether Marlena and I would visit her class of ten students, each of whom had various reasons they didn't fit into the regular classroom routine at Chatelech High School. She wanted us to lead them in storytelling.

On Mondays they met at Kathleen's house, arriving in the school van just before ten. They hung out and played for a few minutes, getting used to the environment, kind of establishing territory.

Kathleen's home held a lively, four-child blended family. The house was well lived in; the students obviously felt comfortable there. As did I, because it was the kind of house I had grown up in, with six brothers and sisters and friends loved to come and hang out.

In the living room, Alicia bent over a complex Lego construction. Tiffany sat on the couch with her eyes downcast. Kyle, tall and rangy, walked restlessly around. When he spotted us in the doorway, he came over immediately and greeted us warmly.

Jesse, smallest in size, was on the big leather couch practising full-body fidgeting. Georgia sat next to Jesse and watched us with open curiosity. Tyrell, big, bulky, brown, silent, with a half-moon smile on his face, watched not just us, not just the room, but something larger and unseen by the others. Evan shambled around on his own, examining his environment, followed by his worker, Carol, who gave him free rein but kept him out of danger and trouble.

We had no idea what differences kept the kids out of regular classrooms. Kathleen and the kids themselves created an ambience that pretty much obviated any sense of difference.

Kathleen asked the kids how they were doing. Alicia was quick, eager to show her Lego construction, a rocket ship with a green dragon at the controls. A monkey sat on the dragon's back. "The monkey is the real pilot, even though it looks like the dragon is."

She paused. "Actually, I have the dragon essence." I wish we would have followed up on that statement.

I had them ask about my face. After I answered, Alicia told me she had not felt comfortable asking. Georgia echoed that, but acknowledged she also wanted to know.

I told about my grandmother grabbing my chin and yelling at me to hold it up and look people in the eye. I told the spin-the-bottle story where I had been rejected by Patty at age twelve, which they loved, especially when I responded to Patty, "You know you want me."

They yelled with delight and Jesse exclaimed, "You are awesome."

Alicia was all over the topic. "I had freckles and I had long hair, too long, down to my waist. I had a birthday party and invited a lot of kids, and only one person came and she was sick and had to leave early. My father was angry and called other parents. But later I got to be friends with popular kids and my life was different. Very different." She talked matter-of-factly, observing and describing her world.

Tiffany wanted to tell her story. "When I was being born"—she gestured with her hand around her neck—"my umbilical cord was around my neck and it choked me. They thought I would die. Two more seconds and I would have died. It was because my father kicked my mother when she was pregnant with me. He did that with my sister too."

Marlena spoke up. "Great story, Tiffany. A story of courage and survival. Right away in your life you had to struggle to survive, and that's why you are strong now. You have a very strong spirit." Tiffany lit up.

Kathleen had been in the kitchen preparing a rhubarb sheet cake for the afternoon snack; she came into the living room and announced that we'd walk to the ocean and eat lunch there. The kids scrambled for lunch bags and boxes and popped out the door, down the road half a mile and down the path through the rainforest to a boulder beach. It was low tide, and the kids got absorbed with the tidepools. Marlena slipped into Alicia's world, clambering with her over the big rocks to secret places, hearing explanations and descriptions of everything found along the way.

I slipped into a bit of a daze sitting in the sun on the warm boulders. The kids became hungry scrambling over the rocks, and lunch was a delightful picnic. Kyle asked whether the cake would be ready to eat when we got back to the house, and all the kids voted yes by acclamation.

They went back to school after lunch; Marlena and I headed home.

I still don't know exactly what we did that day. We were mostly just present with the kids. I don't know whether to say that we fitted in or that they accepted us. I think simply listening gave us big cred.

We returned to similar days several times. Tiffany and Alicia continued to be the storytellers. We got to know Kyle's mother a couple of weeks later; she mentioned that Kyle had told her about us and said we were awesome.

I guess the way to be awesome is to simply be there and to listen.

My New Year's Resolutions

Keep the pencils sharpened.

Lots of live music.

Wear yoga pants that enhance my body parts.

Learn to assess exactly when a bar of soap gets
too small to keep on using it.

Buy a quart of milk at a time rather than a half gallon.

Bathe frequently, especially with Marlena in the tub with me.

Clean the toilets occasionally.

Go to Lyne's yoga class three times a week.

Intend to reorganize desk and working area.

Sit in the Gumboot Café and write.

Make a list of people who love me; review and update daily.

Make a list of people I love; chisel into stone.

Look out the window.

Avoid falling down the stairs.

Make a list.

Continue to be charming and irresistible.

Do not let my tongue hang out.

Develop effective ways of not drooling.

Dance, dance, dance. Bring it, show it, shake it off.

Be a good listener, including listening to myself.

Continue to pick my nose but more discreetly.

Be selectively irritable.

Enjoy an hour of drifting sleep every morning.

Go to bed when tired.

Browse the travel goods section in drugstores.

Picasso

I have long been able to ignore the fact that I have a pronounced facial difference. Most mornings, I don't even bother looking in the mirror. That's what is called denial. Which, for a long, long time, functioned as my version of self-acceptance.

Not long ago, something very different happened. I was learning to video blog and exulting in my new technological sophistication when I saw myself fifteen inches away on my computer screen. A tight shot of my face. All of a brutal sudden I saw myself as others see me when they see me for the first time. With an emotional wrench, I saw myself in all my defective glory.

At first, I did not actually see myself. I did not even recognize what I saw as a human face. I could only focus on one part of what I was looking at. It was like viewing a Picasso painting. The parts did not fit together. A crooked mouth, bulging left cheek, eye too large. A nose in the middle (ah, a familiar reference point). Then the mouth again—askew, chinless. The eye, spotted, like a dog's. Colours as askew as the features. Each part weird, not fitting into a whole. I slipped into a strange combination of attention-deficit and obsessive-compulsive disorders. I had a vague sense of panic. My breathing became shallow, fast. I began to understand that what I was seeing was claiming to be a face, making some sort of crude false attempt to be a face. Distorted, bulging in some places, gaunt in others. I was being forced to believe by this strange thing that it was a face. I was revolted and frightened.

At first I did not know what was behind that face. I certainly did not see it as myself.

Within seconds I became aware that I was looking at my own face. Repulsive. Disgusting. A shock wave went through me.

This all took about ten seconds. When I saw myself, the shame that had been waiting so long, so silently, drenched me. Long-suppressed feelings, dark, inchoate, came pouring out and overwhelmed me. I could not continue blogging. I erased what I had done but could not erase the feelings.

I was ashamed of my shame and did not want to talk about it. A few days later, I was with my writing group, people with whom I had been creative, whom I trusted. I told a lovely co-writer what had happened. I was surprised to hear her say, "Oh, I feel that way every morning."

"Really? *Really?*"

"Oh, yes."

Marlena told me, "Honey, lots of people feel that way. You've been lucky in that you really have found your inner beauty."

Oh yes, I thought. That's right. *I forgot that I tell audiences I had to work hard to find my inner beauty.* Now I was not too sure about that, I was still in shock, even with the kind emotional support from Marlena and friends.

After a few days, the shame and self-pity began to ease. I remembered how many people had confided in me about similar feelings after my performances. I remembered all the ways in which people experience themselves as disfigured.

Those of us who are seen as disabled or in any way inferior—by dint of ethnicity or class or whatever—know what it takes to build and nurture internal strength in the face of the distorted perceptions of others. Is it difficult? Oh yes, often. But you've got to.

Out of my shame, my inner darkness, grew glimmers of understanding. How did that happen? I don't know.

It was hard to believe at the time, but my YouTube encounter with my own face and flaws gave me greater empathy for others—and for myself as well. Now I am better at looking in the mirror.

About the Author

David Roche was recently awarded the Order of Canada for "making Canada and the US a better place" as an advocate for facial difference rights and as an iconic pioneer in disability culture. He has appeared from New Zealand to Moscow to the United Kingdom, and across Canada and the United States (including the White House) as a humourist, solo performer, actor and filmmaker. He is featured in the National Film Board's film *Shameless: The Art of Disability*. He is also an author (*The Church of 80% Sincerity*, Penguin: NY) and most recently, he had a feature role as Otis in *Happy Face*. David loves working with children; he and his wife Marlena produced the educational video *Love at Second Sight* (available at no cost at loveatsecondsight.org).

His presence in the community is as significant as it is on stage, screen, and print. David was a co-founder of the Childcare Switchboard and Single Parent Resource Center of San Francisco, which became a national model. He and Marlena were co-founders of the first massage therapy program in a hospital (Pacific Presbyterian) in the US. And he was a pioneer in 1990 when he stepped on stage alone with a facial difference. David served for years as chair of the board for Kickstart Disability Arts and Culture in Vancouver. He and Marlena live in Roberts Creek, BC, where they are both volunteers for the Sunshine Coast Hospice.